POLITICAL THEORY AND POLITICAL PHILOSOPHY

Seventeen Volumes of Previously Unavailable British Theses

Edited by
MAURICE CRANSTON
London School of Economics and Political Science

A Garland Series

THE SOCIAL AND POLITICAL THOUGHT OF BERNARD MANDEVILLE

Malcolm Jack

Garland Publishing, Inc., New York & London
1987

Copyright © 1987 by Malcolm Jack
All rights reserved

Library of Congress Cataloging-in Publication Data

Jack, Malcolm, 1946–
The social and political thought of Bernard
Mandeville.

(Political theory and political philosophy)
Originally presented as the author's thesis
(doctoral)—University of London, 1974.
Bibliography: p.
1. B. M. (Bernard Mandeville, 1670–1733—
Contributions in political science. 2. B. M. (Bernard
Mandeville), 1670–1733—Contributions in sociology.
3. B. M. (Bernard Mandeville), 1670–1733—Psychology.
I. Title. II. Series.
JC153.M32J33 1987   320'.01   86-27065
ISBN 0-8240-0820-0

All volumes in this series are printed
on acid-free, 250-year-life paper.

Printed in the United States of America

Malcolm Jack

The Social and Political
Thought of Bernard Mandeville

To
all those who have taught me

Contents

	Page
Acknowledgements	1
Preface	ii
Abbreviations	iii
Chapter I The Nature of Man	1
Chapter II Civil Society	30
Chapter III Psychological Individualism	67
Chapter IV Ethics	89
Chapter V Religion	114
Chapter VI Conclusion	131
Appendix I Mandeville The Medical Doctor	136
Appendix II Animal Automatism	143
Appendix III Mandeville The Satirist	151
Notes to Text and Appendices	153
Bibliography Mandeville Canon	192
Primary Sources	195
Secondary Sources	205

Acknowledgements

This work was originally prepared as a doctoral thesis in the University of London in 1974.

Many people have made its appearance possible but I should particularly like to thank my supervisor, Mr Kenneth Minogue, Reader in Politics at the London School of Economics and Political Science, for all his years of patient, critical attention. During the course of my research I had help from various academics and public servants in Holland, Mandeville's country of birth. In particular, I am grateful for the information given to me about his student days at Leiden University by Dr Luyendijk-Elshout, then at the National Museum for the History of Science at Leiden. I should also thank Professor Maurice Goldsmith of Exeter University who acted as my external examiner and always encouraged my incipient 'Mandevilleanism'. Professor Irwin Primer of Rutgers State University made me 'polish' my thoughts somewhat on Mandeville's ethics before he accepted an article for the book of essays entitled Mandeville Studies Martinus Nijhoff, The Hague 1975, which was based on Chapter IV of this work, so he deserves thanks. Lastly I should mention Professor Maurice Cranston of the London School of Economics and Political Science for recommending my work to the publishers, to whom I am also grateful, and Miss Yvonne Pack who has produced the typescript promptly under some pressure.

Needless to say any inaccuracies and mistakes in this book are entirely my own.

London 1985

Preface

The contention of this book is that the thought of Bernard Mandeville can be coherently understood in the light of his psychology. Mandeville believed that human nature determines the structure of society. He contended that by analysing human behaviour, especially motivation, one comes to understand the structure of society, both in terms of its political and economic arrangements.

Mandeville's thought is not systematically presented. The coherency which can be shown to exist in his thinking is an intellectual construction we have to make that links together those subjects - human nature, society and its evolution, politics, religion and the pathology of moral behaviour - in which he was interested.

By undertaking this task of reconstruction, we contribute to the modern re-assessment of Mandeville as a serious thinker whose work influenced the progress of eighteenth century ideas about man-in-society. Mandeville may have started life as a satirist, only concerned with épater le bourgeois - indeed the essayist style of the libertin erudit may be recognized in all his work - but he became more than a mere purveyor of sensational paradoxes. As a mature writer he was, as Hume acknowledged, one of the important early contributors to that 'great science of man', so fruitfully advanced throughout the eighteenth century.

ABBREVIATIONS

Mandeville's Works

(1) Aesop Dress'd — Aesop Dress'd or a Collection of Fables Writ in Familiar Verse, London 1704.

(2) Dion — A Letter to Dion, Occasion'd by his Book Call'd Alciphron, London 1732.

(3) Fable I — The Fable of the Bees, (Ed. F. B. Kaye) Oxford 1924 Vol. I.

(4) Fable II — The Fable of the Bees, (Ed. F. B. Kaye) Oxford 1924 Vol. II.

(5) Female Tatlers — The Female Tatlers, London Nov 1709 - Nov 1710.

(6) Free Thoughts — Free Thoughts on Religion, the Church and National Happiness, London 1720.

(7) Hypocondriack and Hysterick Passions — A Treatise on the Hypocondriack and Hysterick Passions, London 1711.

(8) Mischiefs — The Mischiefs that ought justly to be apprehended from a Whig Government. London 1714.

(9) Oratio Scholastica — Bernard a Mandeville de Medicina Oratio Scholastica, Rotterdam 1685.

(10) Origin of Honour — An Enquiry into the Origin of Honour and the Usefulness of Christianity in War, London 1732.

(11) Stews — A Modest Defence of Public Stews, London 1724.

(12) The Grumbling Hive — The Grumbling Hive: or, Knaves Turn'd Honest, London 1705.

(13) The Virgin Unmask'd — The Virgin Unmask'd: or, Female Dialogues betwixt an Elderly Maiden Lady, and her Niece, London 1709.

(14) Tyburn — An Enquiry into the Causes of the Frequent Executions at Tyburn, London 1725.

CHAPTER I: THE NATURE OF MAN

Bernard Mandeville will not be numbered among the great flatterers of the human species, as he disarmingly shows in this declaration:

'The Beginning of all things relating to Human Affairs was ever small and mean. Man himself was made of a lump of Earth.'[1]

However, he characteristically adds: 'Why should we be ashamed of this?'[2]

Certainly he is not. Like Hobbes[3] before him and Swift in his own time, Mandeville did not idealize human nature; he was never concerned, like Shaftesbury, to present men with a fine ideal to imitate. Rather his concern was to depict men as he saw them, in the world of his day, and this depiction necessarily involved describing 'Fallen Man', a corrupted creature. But analysing human nature, albeit corrupt, never depressed him.[4]

Mandeville shares with Hobbes a basically mechanical view of human nature. He sees man as a machine motivated by his passions[5] and appetites, gratified when he has some measure of success in satisfying them. Thus Cleomenes, Mandeville's spokesman[6] in the Origin of Honour, says:

'All Human Creatures are sway'd and wholly governed by their Passions,[7] whatever fine Notions we may flatter ourselves with, even those who act suitably to their Knowledge, and strictly follow the Dictates of their Reason, are not less compell'd to do so by some Passion or other, that sets them to Work, than others who bid Defiance and act contrary to Both, and whom we call Slaves to their Passions.'[8]

Cleomenes' statement is a universal one and it also contains an element of determination, matters which I shall take up at some length in a later chapter. At the moment I want to remark that Mandeville makes man fundamentally a creature of passions; he subordinates reason to the passions and he suggests an element of self-deceit in man's view of his own behaviour. These are important themes in Mandeville's pyschology which I shall want to explore in this chapter as a prelude to considering what he says about society and its evolution.

Mandeville's concern with man as a creature of his passions is evidenced in his earliest writings, though it is with the 'Remarks', appended to the hudibrastic verse, 'The Grumbling Hive', that we first have sustained essays upon them. In these 'Remarks', Mandeville is concerned to elaborate on the rather meretricious conclusions of his verse, though it is necessary to bear in mind that his satirical intentions[9] were not absent even in these extensions, written, in the first instance, to support the paradox that the 'Vileness of the Ingredients ... together compose the wholesome Mixture of a well order'd Society ...'![10]

The 'Remarks' deal variously with the different passions as they arise in the poem: thus Remark C is on shame, Remark M is on pride, Remark N is on envy and so on. These passions or appetites, for unlike Butler,[11] Mandeville does not distinguish the two, operate on men variously at various times. A modern scholar has said that for Mandeville:

'Man is a compound of passions (desires, appetites) which have been implanted in him by nature, and his actions at any time are to be explained in terms of those of his appetites - fear, anger, lust, pride, envy, avarice - which happen to be uppermost.'[12]

What will arouse the individual passions are external stimuli - Mandeville follows Hobbes in his sensationalist psychology.[13] But the passions themselves are 'innate', they are an integral part of human nature; and examples of human behaviour may be related to them. As he himself says:

'... the Seeds of every Passion are innate to us and no body comes into the world without them. If we will mind the Pastimes and Recreations of young Children, we shall observe nothing more general in them, than that all who are suffer'd to do it, take delight in playing with Kittens and little Puppy Dogs. What makes them always lugging and pulling the poor creatures about the House proceeds from nothing else but that they can do with them what they please, and put them into what posture and shape they list, and the Pleasure they receive from this is orginally owing to the love of Dominion and that usurping Temper all Mankind are born with.'[14]

The passions are thus moving forces which stir men to action. While they lie dormant, nothing of men's talents and abilities will be noticeable, each remaining a mere 'lumpish Machine' which

'may be justly compar'd to a huge Wind-mill without a breath of air'.[15]

When the passions are aroused, they will lead men to action and in the fulfilment which comes from their satisfaction, to pleasure. In a completely 'natural' situation, by which Mandeville means one unfettered by the restrictions of civilised life, men, like other 'untaught Animals', will be concerned only with following the 'bent of their own Inclinations', or with satisfying their natural appetites, regardless of the consequences.[16] In civilised life, or life in society, men will continue to indulge in the satisfaction of their passions but they will do so within the context of certain constraints.

Mandeville's pre-occupation with identifying the 'passionate nature' of man can be clearly understood in the context of a strong literary tradition of French scepticism, as well as with the kind of introspective analysis of English writers like Hobbes, Temple and Locke, with all of whom he was familiar.[17] The French anti-rationalist tradition with which he can be identified began with Montaigne whose *Essays* cast doubt upon the rational element in man's nature and emphasized the inconstancy and fickleness which resulted from the action of his many and contradictory passions.[18] In the seventeenth century these sentiments found an echo in the writings of the *sceptiques* and *libertins*,[19] like de Bergerac, la Mothe Le Vayer, Gassendi and La Rochefoucauld; anti-rationalists like L'Abbadie and La Placette, whose concern was:

'L'Anatomie du coeur en entrant dans le detail des ses passions.'[20]

Most important of all was Pierre Bayle who regarded man as a creature governed by his passions and one whose actions were thereby difficult to reconcile to rational principles.[21] Mandeville has rightly been regarded as a disciple of Bayle[22] and shares this fundamental tenet with him.

Seventeenth and eighteenth writers believed that one passion predominated; Pope exhorted the 'anatomist' to:

'Search then the RULING PASSION: There, alone, The Wild are constant, and the Cunning known; The Fool consistent, and the False sincere; Priests, Princes, Women, no dissemblers here. This clue once found, unravels all the rest ...'[23]

Rochester had felt that fear was the 'ruling' or predominant passion, whilst later, the poet Young, following Milton, spoke of the 'love of fame' as the universal passion.[24] For Mandeville, as for most of the proponents of the French tradition which I have alluded to, the predominant passion was pride or self-love.[25] Mandeville's egoism, a matter I shall return to, was based upon this passion.

In considering Mandeville's understanding of the passion of pride, we have to be aware of a certain change in his views and definitions of it at different stages in his writing. In Part I of the <u>Fable</u>, Mandeville uses the words 'pride' and 'self-love' interchangeably,[26] defining the passion in this way:

'Pride is that Natural Faculty by which every Mortal that has any Understanding over-values, and imagines better Things of himself than any impartial Judge, thoroughly acquainted with all his qualities and Circumstances, could allow him.'[27]

The passion thus consists of the pronounced self-regard each individual has for himself and manifests itself in his 'extraordinary concern'[28] with what others think of him. There can be no doubt that the author of the first part of the <u>Fable</u> understands pride, so defined, as the predominant passion. In the early 'Remarks', Mandeville retains a distinction between pride and shame, the latter being:

'a sorryful Reflexion on our own Unworthiness, proceeding from an Apprehension that others either do, or might, if they knew all, deservedly despise us.'[29]

The desire of men to be thought well of by others is an important part of the passion of pride.

Mandeville proceeds in Part I of the <u>Fable</u> to explore the many ramifications of the passion of pride or self-love as well as of other passions. His consideration of this predominant passion ranges from explaining simpler and more obvious manifestations of vanity, such as is shown in the attention people pay to clothes and outward appearance, to the subtle analysis of the such instincts as maternal affection, of which he says:

'All Mothers naturally love their Children: but as this is a Passion, and all Passions center in Self-Love, so it may be subdued by any Superior Passion, to sooth that same Self-Love, which if nothing had interven'd, would have bid her fondle her Offspring.'[30]

As the predominant passion, self-love or pride is at the centre of Mandeville's scheme of passions and all other passions or appetites may be related to it.[31] In Part II of the Fable, Mandeville introduces a new definition, distinguishing between 'self-love' and 'self-liking'. This occurs in the Third Dialogue between Horatio and Cleomenes where they have been discussing the various manifestations of pride which are acceptable in civil society, like the cultivation of manners, as well as the refinement of styles of living and social rank or what we now call status. Up to this point in the text, Mandeville has continued to use the words he used in Part I of the Fable, namely 'pride' and 'self-love'.[32] He makes the new distinction, for the first time, in the following parts of the dialogue:

'Cleo ... That Self-Love was given to all Animals, at least, the most perfect, for Self-Preservation, is not disputed; but as no Creature can love what it dislikes, it is necessary, moreover, that everyone should have a real liking to its own Being, superior to what they have to any other. I am of Opinion, begging Pardon for the Novelty, that if this Liking was not always permanent, the Love, which all Creatures have for themselves, could not be so unalterable as we see it is.

Hor ... What Reason have you to suppose his Liking, which Creatures have for themselves, to be distinct from Self-love; since the one plainly comprehends the other?

Cleo ... I will endeavour to explain myself better. I fancy, that, to increase the Care in Creatures to preserve themselves, Nature has given them an Instinct, by which every Individual values itself above its real Worth; this in us, I mean, in Man, seems to be accompanied with a Diffidence, arising from a Consciousness, or at least an Apprehension, that we do over-value ourselves. It is this that makes us so fond of the Approbation, Liking and Assent of others; because they strengthen and confirm us in the good Opinion of ourselves. The Reasons why this Self-Liking, give me leave to call it so, is not plainly to be seen in all Animals that are of the same Degree of Perfection, are many. Some want Ornaments, and consequently the means to express it; others are too stupid and listless ...'[33]

Self-love is therefore the general instinct for self-preservation which all creatures are endowed with whilst self-liking is pride,[34] the instinct to seek the applause of other creatures. Self-liking the 'Instinct, by which every Individual values itself above its real Worth',[35] is most developed in civilized society, for:

'Man himself in a savage State, feeding on Nuts and Acorns, and destitute of all outward Ornaments, would have infintely less Temptation, as well as Opportunity, of shewing this Liking of himself, than he has when civiliz'd ...'[36]

Mandeville confirmed his refined definition of these passions in the last of his major works, Origin of Honour, where again the familiar characters of Horatio and Cleomenes are once again discussing human motivation. Horatio sums up:

'I now understand perfectly well what you man by Self-liking. You are of Opinion, that we are all born with a Passion manifestly distinct from Self-love; that, when it is moderate and well regulated, excites in us the Love of Praise, and a Desire to be applauded and thought well of by others, and stirs us up to good Actions: but that the same passion, when it is excessive, or ill turn'd, whatever it excites in our Selves, gives Offence to others, renders us odious, and is called Pride. As there is no Word or Expression that comprehends all the different Effects of this same Cause, this Passion, you have made one, viz. Self-liking, by which you mean the Passion in general, the whole Extent of it, whether it produced laudable Actions, and gains us Applause, or such as we are blamed for and draw upon us the ill Will of others.'[37]

Cleomenes concurs with this opinion and later in the dialogue deliberately corrects the earlier distinction between shame and pride that had been made by Mandeville at the earlier stage of his analysis.[38] That distinction, Cleomenes tells us, arose from an error, to which the author of the Fable 'is willing to own'.[39] The symptoms of exultation in pride and mortification in shame, are, of course, very different:

'but no man could be affected by either, if he had not such a Passion in his Nature, as I call Self-liking.'[40]

The distinction Mandeville eventually makes between self-love and self-liking, is clearly expressed in the French literary tradition I have already mentioned above.[41] In their concern with analysing the passions and particularly the passion of pride, those writers accepted a distinction clearly enunciated by L'Abbadie:

'L'usage de notre langue est hereux ceci, car elle nous fait distinguer entre l'amour propre and l'amour de nous memes. L'amour de nous memes est cet amour, entant qu'il est legitime & naturel. L'amour propre est ce meme amour, entant qu'il est vicieux & corrompu.'[42]

'L'amour de nous meme' is therefore self-love, the natural instinct men have to preserve and look after themselves, whereas 'L'amour propre' is self-liking or pride.[43]

It will be noticed that Mandeville's definition is a slight refinement on this familiar French distinction for in his usage, self-liking is the passion to seek the applause of others 'in general' and it is only odious and called pride when it is excessive or gives offence to others. The added richness of Mandeville's usage is the result of his drawing upon an English tradition which had contemporary expression in the moralizing of writers like Butler, Campbell and Hutcheson. They accepted a similar distinction between that self-love which made men only concerned with the selfish ends and that self-love which made them concerned with the interests of others as well as, or in spite of, their own.[44] This is clear from Hobbes' definition of vain glory as that:

'joy arising from the imagination of a man's own power and ability ... grounded on the flattery of others.'[45]

Mandeville found other sources of inspiration for his emphasis on need that proud men have to seek the approbation of their fellows. Nicole had explained the psychological basis for this craving when he said:

'the very reason why men so passionately covet the approbation of others (is) because it serves so well to confirm and settle them in the good opinion they have of themselves.'[46]

Mandeville entirely accepted this somewhat cynical conclusion though he was aware that anyone's 'good opinion' of himself would vary depending on whom he associated with. Standards would be set within peer groups, an idea Pareto later used when writing about elites. So, Mandeville tells us:

'Children claim the praise of their companions for being disobedient, and theives and burglars without doubt value themselves among their associates for their dexterity of doing mischief ...'[47]

The 'satisfaction of being well thought of' which will be the result of an individual successfully claiming recognition among his fellows, will assuage the pronounced regard each individual has for himself, though it may be necessary, as we shall see later, to disguise this satisfaction in civil society. Nevertheless, satisfying the predominant passion, will be pleasurable for man. Mandeville's psychology is therefore hedonistic.[48]

Although Mandeville clearly identifies self-liking as the 'ruling passion' it is not the only one motivating human beings. He explores the 'operation' of many other passions, including avarice, fear, anger (and forms of courage which arise from it), lust and love, envy and jealousy.[49] Together they make up an extensive 'scheme' of passions which will be used to explain the whole range of human behaviour.

With a mercantilist flourish, Mandeville pronounces avarice, commonly thought of as a vice, as 'very necessary to the Society,[50] for without a strong desire for wealth, trade and all manner of enterprises would not flourish. The 'true Reason why every Body rails so much against it', he says, is, because 'almost every Body suffers by it; for the more the Money is hoarded up by some, the scarcer it must grow among the rest, and therefore when Men rail very much at Misers there is generally Self-Interest at Bottom.'[51]

Moreover, avarice can be of different sorts, either

'that sordid love of Money, and narrowness of Soul that hinders Misers from parting with what they have, and makes them covet it only to hoard up'[52]

or

'a greedy desire of Riches, in order to spend them, and this often meets with Prodigality in the same Persons ...'[53]

The latter mixture seems paradoxical but as in the character of Cataline, it consists of a greed for others' wealth so that the individual can spend it on himself.

Another important passion in Mandeville's psychology is fear, of which he says:

'The Passion that is rais'd in us when we apprehend that Mischief is approaching us, is call'd Fear: The Disturbance it makes within us is always more or less violent in proportion, not of the Danger, but our Apprehension of the Mischief dreaded, whether real or imaginary.'[54]

Fear he says, is proportionate to the apprehension we have of the danger and cannot be shaken off while the apprehension lasts. Nor, like the other passions, can it be controlled by reason, as he explains:

'Those that have been frighten'd will tell you, that as soon as they could recollect themselves, that is, make use of their Reason, their apprehension was conquer'd. But this is no conquest at all, for in a Fright the Danger was either altogether imaginary, or else it is past by that time they can make use of their Reason, and therefore if they find there is no Danger, it is no wonder that they should not apprehend any: But when the Danger is permanent, let them then make use of their Reason, and they'll find that it may serve them to examine the Greatness and Reality of the Danger, and that if they find it less than they imagin'd the Apprehension will be lessen'd accordingly; but if the Danger proves real, and the same in every Circumstance as they took it to be at first, then their Reason instead of diminishing will rather increase their Apprehension.'[55]

Fear, like other passions, cannot be overcome by reason; if it be overcome at all, it will be by another passion, like anger. Indeed, these two passions must be played off against each other by those administering society; for, as living in society will necessitate men giving up some of the demands of their passions, it will lead them to anger and this anger will only be regulable by exciting fear, the fear which attaches to the penalties for breaking societal arrangements, to wit, laws. By this kind of 'dextrous management', politicians and lawgivers, will be able to control the otherwise unruly creature of the passions, man, and they will fully exploit fear,

'The only useful Passion (then) that Man is possess'd of toward the Peace and Quiet of a Society ...'[56]

Fear is also a socially useful passion because it supports religion,[57] an important social prop. Mandeville develops his views about this subject in a full length work, his Free Thoughts, which I shall return to in a later part of this book.[58] At this point it suffices to distinguish two main kinds of fear associated with the religious instinct which Mandeville speaks about - namely the fear of death and the fear of the unknown, or 'futurity'. In the Origin of Honour, where he is talking of the incompatibility of duelling and Christianity, Mandeville alludes to the former of these two fears, as 'the strongest passion in our nature'.[59] Elsewhere Mandeville ascribes the strength of this fear of death to the fact that it conflicts with the 'instinct of Self-Preservation', or self-love:

'In all living Creatures, that fall under our Senses, we perceive an Instinct of Self-Preservation; and the more sensible they are, the greater Aversion they discover to the Dissolution of their Being, Man, the most perfect of them sets an inestimable Value on Life, and knows no Fear equal to the Horror he has against Death.'[60]

This horror can, and has to be, controlled in civil society otherwise there will be no public or private security.

The second of these fears, that of the unknown[61] is particularly strong among savage men in a state of nature, and indeed 'first gives them an Opportunity of entertaining some glimmering Notions of an invisible Power ...'[62]

Mandeville's psychological insight is particularly remarkable in this section of Part II or the *Fable* where he describes the fears which men in primitive societies would have. Savage man would be terrified by:

'Every Mischief and every Disaster that happens to him of which the Cause is not very plain and obvious;'

Indeed, almost everything:

'excessive Heat and Cold; Wet and Drought, that are offensive; Thunder and Lightening, even when they do no visible Hurt; Noises in the dark, Obscurity itself, and every thing that is frightful and unknown, are all administering and contributing to the Establishment of this Fear.'[63]

In the *Origin of Honour*, Horatio and Cleomenes return to this topic. Cleomenes explains how important it is for a ruler to humour fear by ascribing whatever attributes seem appropriate to the 'invisible cause'.[64] So the different religions of the world are explained as political responses to la condition humaine. Mandeville's cynicism does not stop at this for he also wants to limit the altruistic effects that religion, based on fear, may have on men's behaviour in society. While religion bolsters men's 'vows or protestations'[65] and is therefore of essential 'temporal benefit'[66]; it will be tempered by the hypocrisy which is embedded in man's social activity. So the world is full of:

'Men, that to all outward Appearance are Believers, that go to Church, receive the Sacrament, and at the approach of Death are observed to be really afraid of Hell ... yet ... many are Drunkards, Whoremasters, Adulterers, and not a Few of them betray their Trust, rob their Country, defraud Widows and Orphans, and make wronging their Neighbours their daily Practice.'[67]

We should not, then, overestimate the effects of this 'fear of futurity'; its usefulness will depend, as with the usefulness of other passions, on the dexterity with which politicians can manage it.

Among the stronger appetites that Nature has given man, is 'love' or, in its other guise, lust. In the case of 'love' it

'in the first Place signifies Affection, such as Parents and Nurses bear to Children, and Friends to one another; it consists in a Liking and Well-wishing to the Person beloved.'[68] However Mandeville soon goes on to tell us that this love is only another form of self-love. He explains that the reason

'We give an easy Construction to his (the beloved's) Words and Actions, and feel a Proness to excuse and forgive his Faults, if we see any ... (and) his Interest ... make on all accounts our own, even to our Prejudice ...'[69]

is because we

'receive an inward Satisfaction for sympathising with him in his Sorrows, as well as Joys.'[70]

Moreover,

'when we are sincere in sharing with another in his Misfortunes, Self-Love makes us believe that the Sufferings we feel must alleviate and lessen those of our Friend, and while this fond Reflexion is soothing our Pain, a secret Pleasure arises from our grieving for the Person we love.'[71]

The love of another is therefore 'reduced' once more that that self-esteem which is the mainspring of all Mandevillean motivation. Its 'application' also induces pleasure: the operation of the passions leads, in the Hobbesian manner, away from pain, toward pleasure.

A second kind of love, he tells us, is that

'strong Inclination,[72] in its Nature distinct from all other Affections of Friendship, Gratitude, and Consanguinity, that Persons of different Sexes, after liking, bear to one another.'[73]

This is the appetite or passion[74] of sexual instinct which only becomes observable at the time of puberty, although:

'Could we undress Nature, and pry into her deepest Recesses, we should discover the Seeds of this Passion before it exerts itself, as plainly as we see the Teeth in an Embryo, before the Gums are form'd.'[75]

The quotation is interesting in illuminating Mandeville's 'clinical' interest in investigating the passions, reminding us that his is a medical mind applying itself to 'anatomizing'.[76] Nevertheless that medical analysis is set in the context of developing a theory of social psychology, for the sexual instinct has to be sublimated in civil society, otherwise anarchy would result.

Lust is a necessary instinct for the survival of the species as a whole, just as hunger is the appetite which ensures the survival of individuals of the species. Either of these appetites, when thwarted, raise anger in the individual, for anger is 'that Passion which is rais'd in us when we are cross'd or disturb'd in our Desires'[77]

Anger moves men to exert themselves vigorously

'in endeavouring to remove, overcome, or destroy whatever obstructs them in the Pursuit of Self-Preservation ...'[78]

But the situation is made more complicated by Mandeville saying later on:

'what we call Prowess or natural Courage in Creatures, is nothing but the Effect of Anger, and ... all fierce Animals must be either very Ravenous or very Lustful, if not both.'[79]

The chain of reasoning has to be traced back to the 'principle appetites 'of hunger or lust. When man is frustrated in satisfying these appetites, he becomes angry; that anger in turn supports courage,[80] which he terms its 'effects'. The interplay of the passions within the overall 'scheme' is a complex matter.

The last three passions Mandeville considers in the <u>'Remarks'</u> are pity, envy and jealousy; like the other passions they are 'natural impulses' inclining men towards action to satisfy them.

Pity is the same as compassion and

'consists in a Fellow-feeling and Condolence for the Misfortunes and Calamities of others: all Mankind are more or less affected with it; but the Weakest Minds generally the most.'[81]

However, it arises for Mandeville, like Hobbes,[82] from the uneasiness which the suffering of others has upon an individual rather than from any spontaneous, benevolent feeling. So Mandeville says:

'tho' it is the most gentle and the least mischievous of all our Passions, is yet as much a Frailty of our Nature, as Anger, Pride, or Fear.'[83]

There is thus no morally valuable quality about pity as such. Indeed,

'as it is an Impulse of Nature, that consults neither the publick Interest nor our own Reason, it may produce Evil as well as Good. It has helped to destroy the Honour of Virgins, and corrupted the Integrity of Judges; and whoever acts from it as a Principle, what good so ever he may bring to the Society, has nothing to boast of but that he has indulged a Passion that has happened to be beneficial to the Publick.'[84]

When a man saves an innocent child from dropping into the fire he does nothing morally creditable. He merely acts to assuage his own ill feeling as a spectator of pain.[85] Pity is thus an indulgence: it arises from man's value of his own worth; it is rendered entirely parasitic upon that egoism, which I shall show, is central to Mandeville's psychology.[86]

Another passion comprehensible in terms of man's egoism is envy. Envy is:

'that Baseness in our Nature, which makes us grieve and pine at what we conceive to be a Happiness in others.'[87]

Each individual is guided towards pleasure and away from pain by the dictates of self-love;[88] a fellow creature who seems happy suggests our own unhappiness or is a rival to it and thus leads to the stimulation of envy. Envy is a compound of grief and anger; grief at seeing others enjoy what we cannot and anger against them for their enjoyment of it. Like the other compound passion of jealousy, which I shall consider next, envy will have various 'symptoms', appearing at one time in one form and at others in different forms, its degree often being determined by the nearness of remoteness of the objects which give rise to it. The symptoms, Mandeville remarks in medical fashion, are as various as those of the plague and may range from the crude envy of the 'unpolish'd multitude' for the goods and advantages of those better off than themselves, to the refined critical envy of a writer of other men of letters. Even animals, like horses and dogs, exhibit signs of labouring under its sway. In man envy is an important social passion, for it fosters competition and stirs men to emulation.[89] Nevertheless, being a 'compound' passion, envy is difficult to define.[90]

For the same reason the compounds of jealousy, 'Love, Hope, Fear and a great deal of Envy',[91] cannot easily be identified in any given situation. The element of hoping

'is wishing with some degree of Confidence, that the Things wish'd for will come to pass';[92] whilst love, fear and envy we have already considered. Jealousy will thus manifest itself in different forms according to which of its constituent elements dominates. It is at its most painful when love dominates for it is this element which makes men suspicious and angry at those who make them jealous.'[93] An observation of human behaviour has to take account of such complex variables.

Mandeville's passions characterise states of emotions and direct behaviour towards ends. They are part of his mechanical model of human nature based on a Hobbesian theory of repulsion from pain and movement toward pleasure. For he understood men to be 'moved' to action by these passions[94] - one passion only being able to be played off by another one,[95] - rather than by reason. Pride may thus conquer fear[96] or anger take the place of envy.[97] In all such cases a stronger, 'more violent' passion must replace a weaker one.[98] Mandeville's passions are the causes of men behaving in certain ways, they represent, in a set of conditions presumed unchanged, a change in one variable sufficient to account for a change in another variable - ie. in the action undertaken.[99] They describe, as Mandeville himself shows in the following quotation, the 'underlying mechanism'[100] of the human mind:

'in the pursuit of Self-preservation, Men discover a restless Endeavour to make themselves easy, which insensibly teaches them to avoid Mischief on all Emergencies: and when human Creatures once submit to Government, and are used to live under the Restraint of Laws, it is incredible, how many useful Cautions, Shifts, and Stragems, they will learn to practise by Experience and Imitation, from conversing together, without being aware of the <u>natural Causes</u>, that oblige them to act as they do, viz. The Passions within, that, unknown to themselves, govern their Will and direct their Behaviour.'[101]

This passage illustrates Mandeville's interpretation of the passions as underlying 'causes' in 'the mechanism of man' while also bringing to attention another important aspect of his psychology which I have alluded to, namely the way in which men constantly deceive themselves about the motives of their own behaviour and the worth of their actions. This latter feature of psychology I shall call 'cognitive derangement', for it entails an escape into illusion which Mandeville regards as an important factor in the success of man as a social being. Self-deception or derangement takes three main forms in his theory. The first is the blinding of each individual to his own defects, a fact which leads men to over-value their own worth, so that

'the meanest wretch puts an inestimable Value upon himself'.[102]

It is the passion of self-liking which leads men astray in this particular instance, making men, as Butler observed, extremely bad judges in their own cases.[103]

A second feature of 'cognitive derangement' is man's ability to keep hidden from himself the real motives for his actions, an idea Mandeville explores in all his writing.[104] It is given clear expression in <u>Fable II</u> where Cleomenes says:

'I believe moreover, that a Gentleman so accomplished, all his Knowledge and great Parts notwithstanding, may himself be ignorant, or at least not well assured of the Motive he acts from.'[105]

When Horatio protests that his seems unlikely in a man of 'so much Sense, Knowledge and Penetration',[106] Cleomenes offers two reasons why it should be so. The first reason is that over-valuing of each person's worth by himself which we have identified as the first feature of 'cognitive derangement. The other reason Cleomenes offers is 'that if the Person in question was capable of examining himself, it is yet highly improbable, that he would ever set about it: For it must be granted, that in order to search into ourselves, it is required, we should be willing as well as able; and we have all the Reason in the World to think, that there is nothing, which a very proud Man of such high Qualifications would avoid more carefully, than such an Enquiry: Because for all other Acts of Self-denial he is repaid in his darling Passion; but this alone is really mortifying, and the only Sacrifice of his Quiet, for which he can have no Equivalent.'[107]

Mandeville's second feature of 'cognitive derangement' therefore suggests the operation of 'causes', unrecognized or suppressed by individual man, in the conduct of human behaviour that are not unlike promptings of the Freudian subconscious. Suppressed because it is painful for an individual to contemplate his true nature and thereby sacrifice his quiet; these motives must be understood by those aspiring to knowledge or control of man-in-society.

A third feature of 'cognitive derangement' is Mandeville's extension of the Baylian idea of an inconsistency in human behaviour which makes it difficult for man to act consistently according to his principles.[108] This idea is made clear in a passage in the <u>Origin of Honour</u>, where Cleomenes and Horatio are discussing man's fear of death.[109] Horatio remarks that it is the fear of what happens after death which restrains men from certain kinds of behaviour in their worldly life but Cleomenes, now speaking for Mandeville, replies that this is not so. Men certainly do fear death and the beyond but they behave throughout their lives as if they had no thought of any future. Any fear which they might have is superceded by more immediate concerns, like the struggle to survive. The mental make-up of man is therefore such that he cannot act on the logic of his impulse (ie. the fear of death): he has not the constancy to act according to principle.

Mandeville's concern with these ideas of self-deception, or as I have called them collectively, 'cognitive derangement', can be understood against the background of the French heterodox tradition already identified.[110] It is reinforced, in Mandeville, as in Bayle, by that secular Calvinism which saw man as a fallen creature, incapable of rising to the angelic or divine heights of rational behaviour.[111] Nevertheless we find its constituent elements expressed by most of the <u>libertins erudits</u> of seventeenth century France. Thus L'Abbadie notes that pride which leads to the individual's over values of himself:

'L'orgueil n'est que l'enyurement de l'amour propre, qui nous represente a notre imagination plus grans et plus parfaits que nous ne sommes.'[112]

La Placette similarly outlines the deceptive quality of 'amour propre' in the following passage:

'Il nous deguise à nous memes, & fait que nous nous conoissons beacoup moins que nous ne conoissons le reste des choses. Il nous attribue des qualites que nous n'avons pas, on que nous na'avons que dans un degre inferieur à celui ou nous nous imaginons de les avoir. Il nous persuade que nous sommes exempts de plusieurs defaut que nous avons en effet. Il exterme, & reduit a rien ceux que nous ne pouvons nous cacher. Enfin il nous fait croire que nous meritons beaucoup de louange pour des qualites et des avantages que nous posse dans la verite, mais qui ne sont dignes l'aucune estime, n'etant ni les causes, ni les effets, ni les marques meme du merite.'[113]

The concern of these writers and of Mandeville himself with the way in which humans may deceive themselves is part of their wider view of man as basically a creature of his passions rather of his reason. It is a view that places them outside of the important grand rationalist orthodoxy[114] of the eighteenth century which had developed from the natural law tradition, synthesized with seventeenth century science and mathematics. In the medieval tradition of natural law[115] reason was thought to permeate the universe and to govern the relationships between God, Nature and Man. The rational structure of the universe could be understood by man, the only rational animal. This undertanding might come about if man could comprehend the laws of nature, in Montesquieu's later phrase, 'the necessary relations which derive from the nature of things.'[116] Natural laws were understood both as the principles by which events were enacted in the physical universe and the moral embodifications of divine will. The rational and the moral were thus inseparable, even God found their relationship a necessary one:

'If God conforms to the moral law, he is wise and good: if he obeys his own arbitrary will, he is neither the one nor the other; his distinction between good and evil is determined by mere caprice.'[117]

The rationalism inherent in the natural law tradition received further support from Cartesianism, which, paradoxically starting with an expression of extreme scepticism (the doubting of everything except the doubter's thought) ended with a strong assertion of the rational nature of reality. Newton's contribution was to present the picture of a universe that could be understood in mathematical terms, whilst Locke emphasized the special position which man, as a rational being, could enjoy in perceiving the:

'Order, Harmony and Beauty which is to be found in Nature.'[118]

The theological expression of this modern rationalism was in the argument from design. The patterned order and symmetry to be found in nature was interpreted as an expression of divine reason. Ray, an eloquent spokesman of this argument, expressed it in this way:

'the celestial or heavenly bodies, the equability and constancy of their motions, the certainty of their periods and revolutions, the conveniency of their order and situation argue them to be ordained and governed by wisdom and understanding, yea so much wisdom as man cannot easily fathom or comprehend: for we see, by how much the hypotheses of astronomers are more simple and conformable to reason, by so much do they give a better account of heavenly motions.'[119]

The tradition of French sceptical literature to which I have alluded challenged this rational orthodoxy both on philosophical and psychological grounds; philosophically in denying the possibility of attaining knowledge through reason and psychologically in denying that notion of man as a primarily rational being. Montaigne might be called the father of this modern scepticism since in his _Essays_ and especially in _Raimond Sebond_, he cast grave doubts upon the efficacy of reason to uncover truth. The seventeenth century also saw a considerable revival of interest in classical scepticism; Gassendi challenged Descartes' conclusion on the rationality of the universe and became champion of the new school of pyrrhonists.[120] Mandeville was well read in this literature and publicly acknowledged his debt to Pierre Bayle, one of its leading protagonists.[121]

But French scepticism was not the only source of Mandeville's anti-rationalist views. The British empirical tradition was itself prejudice against the more speculative tendencies of Cartesian rationalism. Newton, for all his commitment to mathematics, encouraged validation by experiment. Mandeville, moreover, was influenced by an empirical approach to medical science which Locke and Sydenham did a good deal to encourage in England.[122] His consistently empiricist attitude to learning, is repeated over and over again as was his hostility to a priori reasoning:

More useful Knowledge may be acquired from unwearied Observation, judicious Experience, and arguing from Facts à posteriori, than from the haughty Attempts of entering into first Causes, and reasoning à priori.'[123]

It is especially interesting that Mandeville's rejection of rationalism had such a marked effect on his psychology. He tells us, in language which later found echoes in Hume, that we are

'ever pushing our Reason which way so ever (we) feel Passion to draw it, and Self-love pleads to all human Creatures for their different Views, still furnishing every individual with Arguments to justify their Inclinations.'[124]

However, although I have been concerned to show how Mandeville's view of human nature places him outside the orthodoxy of eighteenth century rationalism, his empirical view of reason and indeed interest in human nature can be understood as a secularized version of natural law, as it was beginning to be understood by the empiricists who followed in the wake of the sensationalist psychology of Hobbes and Locke.[125] These writers were interested in natural law, but 'by nature they came to mean more and more not universal cosmic nature and universal human nature reflecting the inner order and harmony of the universal frame of things - but common human nature as it manifests itself in the passions, motives and actions of individual men and women.'[126]

The laws of nature which they had in mind were psychological laws and 'their method of ascertaining these laws, were the empirical ones of appeal to common experience and observation of the ways of the mind.'[127]

The culmination of this type of analysis is Hume's <u>Treatise of Human Nature</u> and it is interesting and significant that he there cites Mandeville as one of those

'late philosophers in England, who have begun to put the science of man on a new footing ...'[128]

In having this interest in 'common human nature', Mandeville certainly did not share the optimism of writers like Shaftesbury who continued the older natural law tradition, with its belief in natural benevolence, as well as in natural reason.[129] Indeed Mandeville's view of Nature is a grim one. If Nature was not directly hostile to man's progress, it was at any rate indifferent to it and much of human achievement had been a result of ingenuity and effort on man's own part. He tells us:

'There is nothing Good in all the Universe to the best-designing Man, if either through Mistakes or Ignorance he commits the least Failing in the use of it; there is no Innocence or Integrity that can protect a Man from a Thousand Mischiefs that surround him: On the contrary everything is Evil, which Art and Experience have not taught us to turn into a Blessing.'[130]

That man has achieved things and learnt to turn evil to his own advantage by 'Art and Experience', is, of course, providential, but it is the providence of a severe natural order. In that fearsome universe:

'Nothing is more common to Nature, or more agreeable to her ordinary Course, than that Creatures should live upon one another: The whole System of animated Beings on the Earth seems to be built upon this: and there is not one Species, that we know of, that has not another that feeds upon it, either alive or dead; ...'[131]

Such a description certainly betokens order and provision, as he remarks with the case of fish, where an abundance of species are provided so that there is enough food for others to feed off,[132] but it is nevertheless a very different picture of natural 'design' illustrated by Ray.[133] The very harshness that Mandeville depicts is a condition for survival; indeed it is the case that if

'the ill of one private system be the good of others; it makes still to the good of the general system (as when one creature lives by the destruction of another, one thing is generated from the corruption of another; or one planetary system or vortex may swallow up another) then is the ill of that private system no real ill in itself; more than the pain of breeding teeth is ill in a system or body which, without the occasion of pain, would suffer worse, by being defective.'[134]

Moreover within this bleak system of providence, Madevillean Man is himself a corrupt and flawed creature - a truly Augustinian view, and one which places Mandeville in the camp of the 'realists' That group included Hobbes, the French sceptical writers, Swift, Gibbon and Burke and their views may be contrasted with those of the 'idealists' like Cumberland, the Cambridge Platonists, Locke and Shaftesbury who retained a belief in man's rational capacities.

Making man a creature of his passions did not mean that Mandeville expected all men to behave in the same way. Like a good many other eighteenth century writers he took it for granted that human nature remained constant in the sense that it always exhibited the same characteristics through the ages.[135] Indeed this belief, that 'manners and customs may change but human nature is much the same in all ages.'[136] was the basis of the hope that it would be possible to have a science of man in the way that Hume wished in the <u>Treatise on Human Nature</u>.[137] But he was not suggesting that individuals reacted in the same way. Horatio's words in the Third Dialogue of Part II of the <u>Fable</u> make this clear:

'according as men differ in natural Temper, and turn of Mind, so they are differently influenced by the same passion.'[138]

Moreover not only do different men behave differently under the influence of the same passions, but there are differences in behaviour when the passions operate within civil society.[139] I shall consider in the next chapter the various understandings which Mandeville had of the 'state of nature' but it is sufficient here to suggest that at least part of this understanding involved seeing the psychological condition of man outside the sophisticated restraints of eighteenth century European societies.

Mandeville makes clear that he understands an evolution[140] in man as a social creature - the habit of speech[141] is acquired by experience and reason itself is not an endowment but a practical acquisition. These developments come about because man lives in society and subjects himself to its arrangements.[142] Although within the structure of these societal arrangements, man may achieve a satisfaction of his passions, this is not without a certain amount of intelligent planning,[143] or in Mandevillean language, 'dextrous management.' The vital function of organising and maintaining society is carried on through political and legal processes, vigilantly supervised by politicians and lawgivers. They must work upon the 'raw material' of human nature; they must harness men's energy to the cause of society. But it is not in the power:

'of Politicians to contradict the Passions or deny the existence of them, but ... when once they have allowed them to be just and natural, they may guide Men in the indulgence of them, as they please.'[144]

The psychological difficulties between man in and outside society, can, according to Mandeville, be seen in the differences of behaviour between adults and children. Among children, the passions operate in an unrestrained manner and the process of education,[145] which he considers in some detail in the first Part of the Fable, consists in the learning of those restraints individuals must place upon their passions in order to live in civil society. His awareness of the gradualness of the process of education from childhood to adulthood is matched by an awareness of the evolutionary nature of social change. Mandeville criticized those writers like Temple, who underestimated the differences which such evolution brought about and ascribed the psychological characteristics of civilized man to savages.[146]

The difficulty and slowness of socialization was, for Mandeville, a reflection of the great difficulty of controlling human nature, that is, of regulating the passions. Like Hobbes, though with less sanguinity about a prudential solution to problems of conflict, he regarded politics as problematical. Political leaders required great skill:

'To preserve Peace and Tranquility among Multitudes of different Views, and make them all labour for one Interest, is a great Task; and nothing in human affairs requires greater knowledge, than the Art of Governing.'[147]

Because the equilibrium which successful politics achieves is based upon human nature, elements of caprice and chaos threaten the order; there is a fragility in all social arrangements. Mandeville's sensitivity to the precariousness of institutional forms is shown in several of his 'projectionist' tracts, like Tyburn and the Stews.[148]

Mandeville's view of human nature is a 'base' rather than a 'beautiful' one.[149] Although he did not share in the more facile optimism of Shaftesbury and the benevolentists, he did, like Defoe, have considerable pride in the achievements of his own society.[150] Man's ingenuity was the more remarkable in the setting of a hostile, natural environment. The evolution of civil society must now take our attention.

CHAPTER II: CIVIL SOCIETY

'Wise Men', Cleomenes tells us, in a dialogue in Part II of the <u>Fable</u>

'never look upon themselves as individual Persons, without considering the Whole, of which they are but trifling Parts in respect to Bulk ...'[1]

These words of Cleomenes describe Mandeville's principle that society is a collectivity of component units, men of passion, with the psychological characteristics which I we have already considered. Society is the totality of such individuals acting in relationship to one another. The growth and maintenance of society, are for him, psychological processes concerning the adaptation of individuals to social ends. Particular political or economic arrangements have to been seen against this background of psychological individualism.

Mandeville's account of society is given in the traditional language of natural law theory, postulating a progress from the 'state of nature' to 'civil society'. But he imports to his analysis a psychological slant more pervasive than had hither to characterized such social theory. I shall approach his explanation of the origin of politics with that nuance very much in mind.

Mandeville, like Hobbes, considered the condition of the life of man outside civil society, and his view of the state of nature was also distinctly gloomy and foreboding.[2] In such a state, which he interprets quasi-historically but mainly conjecturally, man has neither control of himself nor of his environment, pulled this way and that as he is by blinding passion and chance happening. Mandeville's understanding of the state of nature was 'conjectural' in the sense that he understood it to be the state man would be in without the constraints of (political) society, embodied in civil law. The state of nature is an abstraction, commonly used in seventeenth and eighteenth century political theory as a device for considering questions of human psychology and political obligation.[3] Thus Mandeville tells us in the <u>Preface</u> to the <u>Fable</u> that he wishes to

'examine into the Nature of Man, abstract from Art and Education'[4]

Later, when introducing the 'Remarks', he reminds us that his concern is to portray 'neither Jews nor Christians'; but mere Man, in the State of Nature ...'[5]

But it is in Part II of the <u>Fable</u> that his methodology is most clearly enunciated. There he tells us that:

'By diligently observing what Excellencies and Qualifications are really acquired, in a well-accomplish'd Man; and having done this impartially, we may be sure that the Remainder of him is Nature. It is for want of duly separating and keeping asunder these two things, that Men have utter'd such Absurdities on this Subject; alledging as the Causes of Man's Fitness for Society, such Qualifications as no Man ever was endued with, that was not educated in a Society, a civil Establishment, of several hundred Years standing.'[6]

Mandeville gives a characteristically shrewd psychological explanation for man's reluctance to contemplate his origins, saying:

'When Men are well-accomplish'd, they are ashamed of the lowest Steps, from which they rose to that Perfection; and the more civiliz'd they are, the more they think it injurious, to have their Nature seen, without the Improvements that have been made upon it.'[7]

This reliance on psychological explanation, can at times, make him careless of historical perspective. So he says, rather airily:

'When I have a Mind to dive into the Origin of any Maxim or political Invention, for the Use of Society in general, I don't trouble my head with enquiring after the Time or Country, in which it was first heard of, nor what others have wrote or said about it; but I go directly to the Fountain Head, human Nature itself, and look for the Frailty or Defect in Man, that is remedy'd or supply'd by that Invention: When Things are very obscure, I sometimes make Use of Conjectures to find my Way.'[8]

Mandeville is particularly anxious to dispel the 'absurdities that Men have utter'd'[9] on these matters. Failing to distinguish the different characteristics of civilized and natural man has lead to profound misjudgement about the nature of society even by writers as distinguished as Sir William Temple.[10] The result is a considerable devaluation of their social theory.

One of the analogies Mandeville uses to indicate what we might expect of man in the state of nature, is childhood, a period of life when men are only indirectly subject to social restraints. He sees childhood as a period during which the unrestrained, passionate nature of man is disciplined so that the human being becomes prepared for social life. Childhood is thus a condition of social irresponsibility: should men not be weaned from it, society itself would never be possible. Mandeville does not, therefore, join Rousseau[11] in lamenting Emile's progress from a 'savage' state: rather he would hasten it.

Another analogy which Mandeville used for describing the conditions of man in the state of nature was the common eighteenth century one of 'Savage Man'. This involved considering man in a state of primitive life, without cultural or political refinement.

It occurs in one of his earliest works, the Female Tatler,[12] and approaches more nearly an anthropological understanding of what the life of men in probable (ie. historical) societies might have been. Like other contemporary writers, he is aware of the newly-discovered 'primitive' societies of Africa and America and uses them as illustrations of the early conditions of all societies. Mandeville clearly has little favour for the 'primitive' conditions of life in such societies; in the Female Tatler Lucinda mouths his sentiments:

'when I ... compare the meanness as well as the ignorance of the infant world, and yet unpolished nations of Africa and America, to the knowledge and comforts of human life, which the more civilized countries, and more especially the politer parts of Christendom, enjoy, I can never forbear thinking how infinitely we are indebted to all those that ever invented anything for the publick good: it is they that actually have melioratd their kind, and from that grovelling state and despicable condition in which we now see the Negroes and other savages, raised their posterity to the enjoyment of those blessings we have among us.'[13]

When Horatio, in the Fable, describes a Hobbesian condition of the strong swallowing up the weak, Cleomenes answers:

'What you say agrees exactly with the Accounts we have of the unciviliz'd Nations, that are still subsisting in the World; and thus Men may live miserably many Ages.'[14]

Mandeville therefore attempts to give flesh, in the form of such 'empirical' accounts as were available to him, to the skeletal notion of the state of nature which he and other eighteenth century theorists inherited from the natural law tradition. There is some historical sense[15] to his speculations, but they are vague in terms of time span as the following quotation shows:

'But to commence from Savages, Men I believe would make but small Progress in good Manners the first three hundred years. The Romans, who had a much better Beginning, had been a Nation above six centuries, and were almost Masters of the World, before they could be said to be a polite People.'[16]

We should not take Horatio's guess at time too literally, for Mandeville is at pains to point out in other parts of the 'Dialogues' that the process toward civilized life is a very slow and gradual one;[17] The historical dimension that does insinuate itself into his account is always tentative and never pursued with any rigour.

Whether conjectural or historical, however, there is no doubt that for him, 'the state of nature' is a highly unattractive condition, a time of 'uncontrolled liberty',[18] necessarily anarchic and unsafe, contrasting strongly with the benefits of civilized life. For without the constraints of civil society, 'mere' man follows the impulse of his nature and is directed by

'that natural Instinct of Sovereignty, which teaches Man to look upon everything as centring in himself, and prompts him to put in a Claim to every thing, he can lay his Hands on.'[19]

Moreover natural man

'would have everything he likes, without considering, whether he has any Right to it or not; and he would do everything he has a mind to do, without regard to Consequence it would be of to others; at the same time that he dislikes every Body, that, acting from the same Principle, have in all their Behaviour not a special Regard to him.'[20]

There is thus no moral sense and little prudence in the state of nature. Man would have no regard for the interests or even existence of other men and he would feel obliged to no authority. Despite the uncertainty and precariousness of his life, he would be unable to make or maintain any contract, for

'no Man would keep a Contract longer than that Interest lasted, which made him submit to it.'[21]

Notions of right and wrong, of property and law have therefore no existence in the Mandevillean state of nature - they are acquisitions of civilized society. Because this is so, life in this state is, in the Hobbesian manner, extremely bleak - Natural Man is a pathetic figure, bereft of understanding, language, laws and government; he lives in constant fear of attack by both wild animals and hostile members of his own species. He is plagued by an anxiety not to offend those invisible powers he believes control his fate. His life is that of an animal of feeble physical resources,[22] erratic and insecure.

The life of natural man has to be understood in the context of that grim providence which we considered in the previous chapter. There is no security, physical or moral, for man in that system: he struggles to liberate himself from its dangers by supreme efforts of courage and ingenuity. Mandeville's view of 'The whole system of animated Beings on Earth'[23] suggests an extreme harshness from which, by a process of evolution, man has emerged as a successful social being. The potential for life in society exists in human nature, but its realization depends on a process of trial and error and is subject to long epochs of time. The parallel with Darwin's biological application of evolutionary theory is apparent and it has been argued by F.A. Hayek that Mandeville may be seen as belonging to a long tradition of evolutionary writing culminating in Darwin.[24]

Nevertheless the development of Mandeville's social theory can also be read in a more traditional way, as a 'secularized version of natural law'.[25] For Mandeville the important laws were the psychological laws governing man's behaviour and development; the sytem of providence, the physical environment in which these laws operated. Certain laws of physical behaviour also proved providential, for man's career as a political animal. One of these was the natural tendency men had for avoiding areas of extreme climate where the most dangerous animals would threaten their lives.[26] These lucky aids to man's adaptation to social life mostly provided negative support to his progress: without them social life would be impossible. But they did not amount to sufficient conditions for his living in society: the extra impetus had to be found in the internal stimulus, or motivation, that drove man to seek the life of communities.[27]

The balance between the potential provided by the system of Providence and man's own achievement is well illustrated in Mandeville's comments on man's sociability, a much discussed topic among seventeenth and eighteenth century political and social theorists.[28] The matter arises most acutely in a Dialogue between Horatio and Cleomenes in Part II of the <u>Fable</u> where, after an evasion, Cleomenes answers Horatio's question as to whether man was, by nature, 'designed for society', with the following words:

'Nature had design'd for Man for Society, as she had made Grapes for Wine.'[29]

When Horatio remarks that wine is an invention of man, Cleomenes adds:

'And so it is to form a Society of independent Multitudes; and there is nothing that requires greater Skill.'[30]

The earlier metaphor is then analysed in terms of the balance between what is providentially given, that is the fitness of man for society as the fitness of grapes for wine; and what is added, the 'Concurrence of human Wisdom',[31] an accumulation of social and political skill. Mandevillean Man is therefore only sociable in a qualified sense, in the sense, that is, that he has potential for life in society. His real sociability arises only after he has lived in society. The actual scope for expression of his sociability is only to be found in society when he has come to discern the advantages of living with his fellow men.[32]

The passions which particularly contribute to the potential for social life among men are self-liking and fear, tempered by understanding. For without fear, of other men as well as of wild creatures, Man would 'never ... be govern'd'[33] and without government there would be no society. Understanding[34] enables man to find a way of calming his fear, but paradoxically:

'the same Superiority of Understanding in the State of Nature, can only serve to render Man incurably averse to Society, and more obstinately tenacious of his Savage Liberty, than any other Creature would be, that is equally necessitous.'[35]

We appreciate this puzzling conclusion better if we consider how understanding actually contributes to man's sociability. In the first place, it makes him more 'sensible of grief and joy',[36] being able to experience these with much more subtlety than other creatures. Furthermore understanding makes man 'more industrious to please himself', contributing to the adaptability of the human animal in being able to know how to acquire what he wants. Finally it 'gives us a Foresight, and inspires us with Hopes, of which other Creatures have little, and that only of things immediately before them'[37]

However, these effects of understanding render man competitive and aggressive in a state of nature. That is because they are untempered by the realization that some degree of co-operation with other men is necessary to survive: the struggle of each individual to gain his ends is unrestrained and fierce. In civil society, these qualities contribute to an individual's well being for the condition in which he struggles to achieve his goals are socially regulated.

Mandeville's emphasis on the transformation that takes place between nature and society is, of course, politically inspired. Though he no doubt adhered to what he believed was the psychological truth of his account, he was also anxious to stress the benefits of social life to his readers. What is more he wanted to 'educate' that minority of them who will be leaders into the difficult art of government which must begin with an understanding of human nature.

Having given us these views about sociability, Mandeville has still, in the eighteenth century manner, to account for the origin of society. This he does with some subtlety in the dialogues of Part II of the <u>Fable</u>. He begins by saying that self-love, the instinct man has to preserve himself, will make man 'scrape together'[38] what is necessary for survival with some degree of security for himself and his children. The family origin[39] of social instinct is stressed for

'Man will look upon his Children as his Property, and make use of them as is most consistent with his Interest.'[40]

The family becomes the means by which each man may satisfy his predominant passion, that self-liking or instinct to bask in the glory of applause.[41] Family members provide the most obvious forum for satisfying his need for approval. Savage or 'untaught' man:

'would desire that everybody that came near him, to agree with him the in the Opinion of his Superior Worth, and be angry, as far as his Fear would let him, with all that should refuse it; He would be highly delighted with, and love every body, whom he thought to have a good opinion of him, especially those, that by Words of Gestures should own it to his Face ...'[42]

Those 'nearest' him, ready to 'own' their good opinion to his face, would be the closest members of his family.

However, family relationships would not be necessarily complimentary at all times. The natural affection of a parent for a child and the opportunity the presence of his child would present for the gratification of his self-liking would not be the only factor affecting their relationship. As we have already seen, Mandevillean man is a creature in whom various passions operate in different degrees of strength. Though the parent will be swayed by the 'reconciliatory' emotion of self-liking, he will also succumb to the 'alienating' passion of anger. Thus if the offspring of Natural Man defies him, he is liable to be roused to anger and may even physically assault his child, only falling under the influence of his natural affection for the child when remorse has set in and shown him the harsh results of his anger.[43]

Mandeville develops his account of the relationship between the 'savage' parent and child by saying:

'now if we consider, that all Creatures hate and endeavour to avoid Pain, and that Benefits beget Love in all that receive them, we shall find, that the Consequence of this Management would be that the Savage Child would learn to love and fear his Father: These two passions, together with the Esteem, which we naturally have for every thing that far excels us, will seldom fail of producing that Compound, which we call Reverence.'[44]

Mandeville hints at the initial conditions for social life in these words, for the submission of the child to his parent implies governability. Nevertheless he does not want to rush to his conclusion. The evolution of society is a gradual process that will take centuries to achieve: the transition from natural to civil life is a long process, subject to reverses. Cleomenes replies to Horatio's rather artful naivety in seizing upon parental authority as a basis for government by saying:

'I thought you would go too fast. If the wild Man had understood the Nature of Things, and had been endued with general Knowledge, and a Language ready made, as Adam was by Miracle, what you say might have been easy; but an ignorant Creature, that knows nothing, but what his own Experience has taught him, is no more fit to govern, than he is fit to teach the Mathematicks.'[45]

To assume that government could result so quickly, would be, in Mandeville's view, committing the fallacy of ascribing characteristics of civilized men to savages, an accusation he had levelled against other writers, notably Temple.[46] Uneasy and unstable family groups would continue for long periods of time; savage man would act capriciously and he would want the foresight to establish rules so that inter-family relations could be stabilized. Before further progress toward society could be properly made, Mandeville considered that certain exterior pressures would have to work upon men and at least on vital invention would have to be made.

The first of these pressures would be the need for greater organisation and defence of the family in view of the threat of wild animals. Horatio summarizes it in this way:

'I plainly see, that Mankind might subsist and survive to multiply, and get the Mastery over all other Creatures that should oppose them; and as this could never have been brought about, unless Men had assisted one another against Savage Beasts, it is possible, that the Necessity Men were in of joining and uniting together, was the first Step toward Society.'[47]

Cleomenes later in the dialogue confirms that he

'can find no Cause or Motive, which is so likely to unite them (men) together, and make them espouse the same Interest, as that common Danger they must always be in from wild Beasts, in uncultivated Countries; whilst they live in small Families, that all shift for themselves, without Government or Dependence upon one another; This first Step to Society, I believe to be an Effect, which that same Cause, the common Danger so often mentioned, will never fail to produce upon our Species in such Circumstances ...'[48]

However the life of men in family groups with some kind of commonly organized defence against wild animals, would become difficult when the common danger diminished. Cleomenes again explains:

'If we consider, that Strength, Agility, and Courage would in such a State be the most valuable Qualifications, and that many Families could not live long together, but some, actuated by the Principle I named, (of 'Pride and Ambition, that all Men are born with') would strive for Superiority: this must breed Quarrels, in which the most weak and fearful will, for their own Safety, always join with him, of whom they have the best Opinion.'[49]

Man would therefore leave the state of nature for some intermediate state, identifiable as fully fledged social life. In such a condition 'Men may live miserably many Ages'[50] and indeed it is a state of affairs that 'agrees exactly with the accounts we have of the unciviliz'd Nations, that are still subsisting in the World ...'[51]

During this period of social anarchy during which the fragile family groupings would struggle to survive, the second important pressure upon men to form a more coherent society would become apparent, namely the fear which they had from each other.[52] Generations,[53] of strife would cause:

'human Nature to be look'd into, and begin to be understood: Leaders would find out, that the more Strife and Discord there was among the People they headed, the less use they could make of them:

this would put them upon various ways of curbing Mankind; they would forbid killing and striking on another; the taking away by force the Wives, or Children of others in the same Community: they would invent Penalties, and very early find out, that no body ought to be a Judge in his own Cause; and that old Men, generally speaking, knew more than young.'[54]

The fear men had of destruction at the hads of rival family groups[55] would eventually lead to the establishment of rules and conventions, the framework of social order, between the scattered communities. However, it would not be possible for these developments to take place without one vital invention, namely that of writing, for in its absence, laws could not be set down, the administrtion of justice could not be formalized and the preservation of social order itself could not be stabilized. The invention of letters is thus, in the Mandevillean account, the third 'step'[56] toward the establishment of society.

Mandeville's three 'steps' towards society describe the conditions without which there could be no social life; they form part of his anthropological account of the progress of man from the state of nature to civil society. But they do not in themselves guarantee the establishment of political order, for they happen to a creature, man, whose sociability is, as we have seen,[57] only potential. This potential has to be exploited, man has to be politically and morally 'managed' before society is possible. The 'steps' toward society show the necessary but not sufficient conditions for the politicization of human life. They are supplemented, in Mandeville's account, by a detailed analysis of the process of socialization or the way in which, through his own ingenuity, man is able to seize the opportunity of social life offered by the accidents of his environment. A certain ambivalence can be traced in this analysis for at times Mandeville stresses the accidental nature of this process (the 'concurrence of many favourable accidents'[58]) and thereby anticipates Scottish enlightenment theorists like Adam, Ferguson and Smith in identifying consequences of human action which are not the intended results of human design;[59] at others his emphasis is on the more explicit, Machiavellian art of manipulation that all princes had to learn.

The Machiavellian art of government is most thoroughly advocated in Mandeville's earlier work, especially in the essay on the 'Origin of Moral Virtue' which was appended to the 1714 version of the <u>Fable</u>. It will be worthwhile exploring that strand in his thought before considering how the two emphases co-exist in his mature work.[60]

The basis on which the political appeal to natural man is made is described in this way:

'The Chief Thing ... which Lawgivers and other wise Men, that have laboured for the Establishment of Society, have endeavour'd, has been to make the People they were to govern, believe that it was more beneficial for every Body to conquer than indulge his Appetites, and much better to mind the Publick than what seem'd his private Interest.'[61]

Self-appointed leaders therefore appeared to persuade men of the advantages of social life by appealing to their <u>amour propre</u>. These 'lawgivers and other wise men'[62] thus 'extolled the Excellency of (our) Nature above other Animals' and taught that pursuit of public good was becoming for such sublime creatures as men.[63] They went further and created a political myth which Mandeville explains in this way:

'To introduce, moreover, an Emulation amongst Men, they divided the whole Species into two Classes, vastly differing from one another: The one consisted of abject, low-minded People, that always hunting after immediate Enjoyment, were wholly incapable of

Self-denial, and without regard to the good of others, had no higher Aim than their private Advantage; such as being enslaved by Voluptuousness, yielded without Resistance to every gross desire, and made no use of their Rational Faculties but to heighten their Sensual Pleasure. These vile grov'ling Wretches, they said, were the Dross of their Kind, and having only the Shape of Men, differ'd from Brutes in nothing but their outward Figure. But the other class was made up of lofty high-spirited Creatures, that free from sordid Selfishness, esteem'd the Improvements of the Mind to be their fairest Possessions; and setting a true value upon themselves, took no Delight but in embellishing that Part in which their Excellency consisted; such as despising whatever they had in common with irrational Creatures; opposed by the help of Reason their most violent Inclinations and making a continual War themselves to promote the Peace of others aim'd at no less than the Publick Welfare and the Conquest of their own Passion.'[64]

These two different 'creatures' would behave very differently and on the basis of their behaviour, a system of moral prescription would be made. Men

'agreed with the rest (of their fellow men) to call every thing, which, without Regard to the Publick, Man should commit to gratify any of his appetites, VICE, if in that Action there could be observed the least prospect, that it might either be injurious to any of the Society, or ever render himself less serviceable to others; And to give the name of VIRTUE to every Performance, by which Man, contrary to the impulse of Nature, should endeavour the Benefit of others, or the Conquest of his own Passions out of a Rational Ambition of being good.'[65]

Mandeville's moral theory will be the subject of a later chapter; but it is relevant at this point to appreciate how conspiratorial is his first presentation of the social compact. With deliberately paradoxical intentions, he insists that what have traditionally been called 'frailties', that is the passions, are the most powerful human agencies, provided they are 'Skilfully managed.'[66] His infamous expression of this heterodoxy appears in the following passage:

'It is visible then that it was not any Heathen Religion or other Idolatrous Superstition, that first put Man upon crossing his Appetites and subduing his dearest Inclinations, but the skilful Management of wary Politicians; and the nearer we search into human Nature, the more we shall be convinced, that the Moral Virtues are the Political Offspring which Flattery begot upon Pride.'[67]

The business of political leaders, the lawgivers and moralists, is thus a psychological exercise, only possible in so far as they come to understand human nature and the manner in which it can be guided or controlled. Psychology is the key to successful government: it has precedence over economics or mere administration.[68]

Moroever the process of controlling men must begin in childhood.[69] In the 'Origin of Moral Virtue', Mandeville considers the example of how little girls are flattered into making good curtsies, while elder ones are told that they have already become grown-ups and should not need the same kind of encouragement, itself another form of flattery. He comments:

'These extravagant Praises would by any one, above the Capacity of an Infant, be call'd fulsome Flatteries, and, if you will, abominable Lies, yet Experience teaches us, that by the help of such gross Encomiums, the young Misses will be brought to make pretty Curtsies, and behave themselves womanly much sooner, and with less trouble, than they would without them.'[70]

The same is true of boys, mutatis mutandis, and in both cases the behaviour arises because:

'The meanest Wretch puts an inestimable value upon himself, and the highest Wish of the Ambitious Man is to have all the World, as to that particular, of his Opinion ...'[71]

Flattery is one method leaders use to cajole men into living in society.[72] But the passions which, in a state of nature, are so injurious to man,[73] gain extra scope within society. Indeed some of man's attributes are so anti-social that Mandeville concludes:

'For if by Society we only mean a Number of People, that without Rule of Government should keep together out of a natural Affection to their Species or Love of Company, as a Herd of Cows or a Flock of Sheep, then there is not in the World a more unfit Creature for Society than Man; an Hundred of them that should be all Equals, under no Subjection, or Fear of any Superior upon Earth, could never Live together awake Two Hours without Quarrelling, and the more Knowledge, Strength, Wit, Courage and Resolution there was among them, the worse it would be.'[74]

It is a measure of the skill needed of political leaders that they have to convert this unpromising creature into a conscientious citizen, capable of contributing to society. Mandeville formally defines society as:

'a Body Politick, in which Man either subdued by Superior Force, or by Persuasion drawn from his Savage State, is becoming a Disciplin'd Creature, that can find his own Ends in Labouring for others, and where under one Head or other Form of Government each Member is render'd Subservient to the Whole, and all of them by cunning Management are made to Act as one.'[75]

In an earlier passage in the 'Origin of Moral Virtue', Mandeville has already made the point that although man may be 'subdued' by 'superior Strength',[76] he cannot be made 'tractable, and receive the Improvements he is capable of' by it; he cannot, in short, be converted to a political animal, except by persuasion. Political leaders[77] have

'To preserve Peace and Tranquility among Multitudes of different Views, and make them all labour for one Interest.'[78]

This is a 'great task',[79] requiring an understanding of individual man precisely enough to

'make every Frailty of the Members as Strength to the whole Body, and by dextrous Management turn private Vices into publick Benefits.'[80]

It involves 'playing the passions off against each other', as well as understanding those self-deceptive qualities of human nature, which I have identified as 'cognitive derangement'.[81] When the art of political management has reached a high level, man wil have been conditioned so thoroughly that he will have

'become ignorant, or at least insensible of the hidden Spring, (the operation of the passions) that gives Life and Motion to all his Actions.'[82]

Mandeville's early political theory is modified, in his later work, by a new emphasis on the gradual evolution of social institutions and although there is a difference in stress, it is an exaggeration to describe them, as one modern critic has done, as 'two major historical accounts of the origins of morals and society'.[83] In his earlier work, which I have just been considering, Mandeville concentrates on the actual process of establishing political control; later he considers the wider anthropological background of social development which precedes and is simultaneous with the establishment of this control. The two accounts are therefore not contradictory but reflect a changed interest on his part.

Even in his earlier exposition of the lawgivers and their creation of the political myth, Mandeville introduces various qualifications which refine his explanation. He warns his reader to see the efforts of the lawgivers against the wider background of his general theory of human nature and not just as an isolated, political occurrence. That general theory explains man as a creature of passions but it also emphasizes the complexity and difficulty of understanding and controlling human nature. The task of the lawgivers and moralists thus becomes a good deal more complicated than at first sight appears (ie. than appears by reading the 'Origin of Moral Virtue' in isolation) and in its presentation as a fable may be seen as a simplified abridgement of what is in fact a complex process.[84] He uses the device of the lawgivers and other wise men to dramatize and abridge his tale but it should not be read too literally or in isolation from all that he has told us about the human condition.

When Mandeville came to write Part II of the *Fable*, published in 1728, his interest had shifted to the process of social evolution and to sketching a conjectural history of the origin of society. It was that kind of 'philosophic history' which became the underlying preoccupation of the Scottish Enlightenment writers like Adam Ferguson and continued to find support even among 'empirical' historians like Gibbon at the end of the century. But Mandeville's shift in emphasis does not mean he had set aside his earlier account of the actual establishment of political society. He still saw a vital role for the political 'cementing' that myth could achieve, but he had expanded and refined his understanding of the long and complex history of man's emergence as an animal capable of political organization.

Moreover both accounts emphasize the psychological nature of Mandeville's concerns, and explain why for him there is no attempt at such quasi-legalistic concepts as the contract in his social theory.[85] The transition from the state of nature to civil society is explained in terms of socio-economic and psychological factors, not in terms of moral or legalistic obligations. Thus Mandevillean Man becomes political because it is the way in which he can best realize his potential, that is, he can indulge with greater safety and satisfaction, 'the multiplicity of his desires'[86] and especially the craving to be well-thought of, the most pervasive form of his self-liking. However in taking the view that men obey the state because in it they can best realize their potential, Mandeville does not, as such, deny the moral links which bind men, as subjects, to the state.[87] He does not, dismiss the importance of the feeling of moral obligation in the sustenance of civic life; indeed, the entire object of those managers of society described as 'lawgivers' and 'moralists', was to instill this sense, the lack of which, Mandeville considered, would perpetuate the anarchic conditions of the state of nature. What Mandeville has done is to give a psychological account of the moral instinct and to insist upon its necessary connection with the passion of self-liking, that seeking of the applause of fellow men which he regarded as a self-evident but empirically verifiable characteristic of human nature.[88] In the 'Body Politick' man can 'find his own Ends in Labouring for others',[89] or in behaving according to the prompting of his moral sense. The moral impulse is therefore an important element in man's sociability; for this reason Mandeville, like any other political theorist, must understand and take account of it. He must also be aware of the conditions in which it can be corrupted.

Mandeville does not, therefore, concern himself with searching for the moral answer to the traditional question of political theorists, namely why men should obey the state.[90] Rather he takes on the task of analyst and indeed pathologist of the body politic. He accepts the need for authority as axiomatic. Men owe obedience to the 'highest magistrate' because without their compliance there would be no government, therefore no order or security and indeed the pitiful conditions of the state of nature, or at best, that

long and 'miserable' period of inter-family war. The actual form
of government[91] concerns him as little as it did Pope: men will
find various patterns of social order to suit the 'variety of
(their) appetites.'[92]

Understanding this approach makes more intelligible
Mandeville's dismissal, in Chapter XI of <u>Free Thoughts</u>, the
traditional search for the best form of government. That quest
had led to constant disagreement, itself injurious to the
continuance of the state. All forms of government suffer
inconveniences,[93] as Pope had said:

> 'For Forms of Government let fools contest;
> Whate'er is best administer'd is best'[94]

Mandeville shares Pope's conservative values of order and
security;[95] he believes that whatever government can achieve and
maintain such ends deserves support from its citizens. In England
these goals are best achieved by a balance in the powers of Kings,
Lords and Commons. This was the traditional Whig theory of
constitution made a commonplace by Locke. Mandeville accepts, in
the conventional manner, the 'happy mixture' of the three elements
of monarchy, aristocracy and democracy in the English constitution.
Parliament is the initiator of laws, while the monarch is their
'guardian and superintendent' and is encharged with 'enforcing and
preserving'[96] their validity. In this political system it is the
law which is supreme and even the monarch is subject to it. When
the King breaks the law, he breaks his contract with his subjects
who are thereby relieved of any obligation to obey him further.[97]

Mandeville accepts the traditional Whig idea of the balanced
constitution, in the neo-Harringtonian[98] style, since it most
nearly leads to the possibility of order and security, of economic
and social progress, free from the despotism and papacy

which he deprecates. In the tract of 1714, Loveright, the Whig apologist, is made to mouth the sentiments:

'A Whig is one that stands up for Liberty and Property and the welfare of the Nation.'[99]

Nevertheless, although Mandeville accepts the facade of Whig constitutionalism, he is not easily identified with party politics in a straightforward way.[100] He says himself that

'I have nothing to do with Whigs or Tories'[101]

and his main political plea is for national unity against 'faction',[102] so that trade and commerce may thrive. This plea becomes more urgent when we consider the 'rage of party' which had brought a violent flavour into Augustan politics.[103] If it is difficult to find Mandeville referring to specific political events or taking a firm stand in party disputes, there can be no doubt that in a general sense he was committed to challenging what has been called the 'political theory of virtue'[104] by his support of emerging commercialism.

Adherents of the 'political theory of virtue' warned of the constitutional and moral corruption that could engulf the state. A dangerous constitutional imbalance had arisen on account of the displacement of the House of Lords as the counterweight to the King and the People. Even more important, however, had been the development of the new commercialism[105] of post-revolutionary England which the 'ideologists' of virtue saw as a corrupting influence. This economic change was based upon money and the acquisition of wealth through business; institutionally it was reflected in the establishment of joint-stock companies and in the setting up of the Bank of England in 1694. With a growth in the importance and influence of the City of London and business interests in general, the bourgeoisie[106] seemed to be a class of increased importance and presented a threat to the traditional social structure of the country, firmly based, as it was, upon landed interest.

Even those aristocrats who took part in the growth of commercial enterprise,[107] could be corrupted. Defoe, in rather bad faith, pretends to lament this in lines that Mandeville would have approved:

'Wealth, howsoever got, in England makes
Lords of merchants, gentlemen of rakes
Antiquities and birth are needless here
'Tis impudence and money makes a peer'[108]

These developments were abhorred by the 'old Whigs' who were steeped in Harringtonian constitutionalism, as well as by the Tories who represented the traditional values of landed society and sought 'the simplicity of pre-revolutionary days'.[109] Societies dedicated to 'reforming manners' were founded. The widespread Augustan notion that English society was corrupt has expression in numerous pamphlets and tracts,[110] like those of Ned Ward and in the critiques of Law, Fielding and Berkeley.[111]

In the **'Patriot King'**, Bolingbroke gave expression to the Tory hope for a return to the 'moral life' of pre-Revolutionary England, based on social hierarchy and landed aristocracy. This was to be achieved under the guidance of the 'supreme magistrate' who would, by his own lofty personal example of disinterested virtue, turn his people away from the sordid pursuit of financial gain. Bolingbroke always turned to ancient Rome for political and moral inspiration: from that example, he drew, as Gibbon was later to do in so celebrated a way, analogies for the future of his own country.

Rome flourished so long as she maintained the highest standards of disinterested public service and while her citizens' primary concern was the common weal. When material luxury became the public and private obsession of her citizens, then her decline had begun and her greatness was endangered. Finally avarice destroyed the very fabric of her society. The 'simple', moral Roman Republic had degenerated into the luxury-loving Empire, which in turn, succumbed to barbarism. This simplified view of the course of Roman history[112] served to re-inforce those protesting against the moral corruption they saw in their own society and it sustained them in their 'prolonged satirical crusade against the degeneracy of the times.'[113]

However, the battle between the 'Republicans' and the new Whigs did not lack elements of personal animosity. Bolingbroke's pronouncements were as much inspired by a dislike of Walpole who represented for him the horror of the political arriviste, as by deep felt moral principles. Before Walpole's ascendency, Swift, a staunch ally and friend of Bolingbroke, had launched a savage attack on Marlborough, the Whig military commander-in-chief, in the Examiner. He had also tried to undermine the position of the war leadership in the Conduct of the Allies, 1711.[114] Swift accused Marlborough of extending the war to satisfy his own prvte ends. It was a charge that may have been an useful excuse for the Tories to demand an end to the war which they wished to see terminated for other reasons.[115] Once Walpole's ascendancy had begun, the element of personal animosity in political life became standard. Swift was the vicious spokesman for the anti-Walpole lobby, describing Walpole as a 'money-grubber' addicted to 'filthy lucre',

> 'A jobber of stocks by retailing false news
> A prater at Court in the style of the stews.'[116]

Bolingbroke himself, in journalistic rather than philosophic vein, did not spare his enemies:

'It hath been the peculiar misfortune of this Nation, especially of late Years, to fall into the hands of <u>such Vultures</u>, who prey upon the Blood and Vitals of their Country. We have seen the most execrable Frauds and Villainies cloaked and perpetuated under the Name of Charity; and a pretended concern for <u>publick good</u> made the Hackny tool and Instrument of <u>private Interest</u> and <u>Corruption</u>.'[117]

Within this context, Mandeville emerges as a defender of doctrines of commercial expansion and Whig constitutionalism. Not only does he see such doctrines as necessary for national grandeur, but they more nearly accord with his theory of man as a creature of his passions. An austere and virtuous republic as Bolingbroke and his friends dreamed of offered little scope for the satisfaction of pride and avarice.[118] It was therefore an unrealistic ideal for any Mandevillean statesman. Although Mandeville did not launch substantially into particular issues, he did make a strong defence of Marlborough in the <u>Fable</u>. In the Dialogue where this is to be found, Mandeville has already minimized the qualities necessary for political leadership, as for example, for prime ministership.[119] He then turned to considering the Opposition view of Marlborough which:

'attributed all his Successes to the Bravery of his Troops, and the extraordinary Care that was taken at Home to supply his Army; and insisted upon it, that, from the whole Course of his Life, it was demonstrable, that he had never been buoy'd up or actuated by any other Principles than excess of Ambition, and an insatiable greediness after Riches.'[120]

Mandeville will have none of this; Cleomenes and Horatio agree that in fact, Marlborough was a 'very great Man, an extraordinary Genius'[121] whose patriotism and concern for national, rather than sectarian, interest, should be recognized and admired. In an earlier work, Mandeville had shown his admiration for William III[122] for similar qualities.

Mandeville's support for the emerging commercialism of Augustan England is strongest in his espousal of certain economic doctrines, notably in his enthusiasm for wealth and in his advocacy of luxury. He began, in the 'Grumbling Hive', with a parody of austerity. The inspiration for this early jeu d'esprit was the satirical possibility of exposing the inconsistency and absurdity of those who demanded (like Bolingbroke and his friends were later to do) a return to some simple pre-Revolutionary life while at the same time insisting on their patriotic interest in forwarding he 'greatness' of their country. In the satire, Mandeville represents society as a hive of bees, whose life is busy and prosperous, until one day Jove answers their repeated pleas for a return to a simple and virtuous life, by granting it to them. With the dawning of a new, virtuous age, the vices of price and avarice disappear from the hive; honesty and frugality become the order of the day. But such an age also brings poverty and backwardness, so that without vices, life becomes severe as well as simple.

Mandeville's fable is thus an ironic retort to all primitivist arguments for a return to 'the simple life'. Men had to choose between 'greatness' and simplicity. While the hive was thriving and busy, it provided the opportunity for the indulgence of passions, especially pride and avarice. When it is reformed, such opportunity disappears. A reformed society may suit saints, it is unlikely to suit men as they are in the world. Anyone who pretends otherwise is a fool or a hypocrite.

Later, in the 'Remarks', Mandeville considered the economic argument more seriously. His twin intention was to discredit frugality and advocate luxury.[123] He began by examining the circumstances of the Netherlands since Sir William Temple[124] had authoritatively argued that Dutch properity arose from a habit of national frugality and England would benefit by practising the same habit. Mandeville rejected this argument entirely, insisting on the essential difference between the economies of the Netherlands and England. According to him, Dutch frugality arose because of very peculiar needs of the Low Countries. These included the expenditure of large sums of public money on the war against the Spanish and additional large amount on combatting the physical hazard of the sea. Neither of these factors applied to England. Moreover, argued the Dutch expatriate doctor,[125] with as much authority as Temple, the geography of the two countries was quite different. The Netherlands lacked the fertility of England, a land altogether 'more happily situated' where men

'are much richer within themselves, and have to the same Number of People, ten times the Extent of Ground.'[126]

Indeed Dutch prosperity had little to do with the actual land. Although the Dutch: 'may ascribe their present Grandeur to the Virtue and Frugality of their Ancestors as they please; but what made that contemptible Spot of Ground so considerable among the principal Powers of Europe, has been their Political Wisdom in postponing every thing to Merchandize and Navigation, the unlimited Liberty of Conscience that is enjoy'd among them, and the unwearied Application with which they have always made use of the most effectual means to encourage and increase Trade in general.'[127]

These are policies which could be carried out in England as well. By advocating them, Mandeville becomes a supporter of the Whig commercialism of the Walpole era.

However, the most controversial doctrine Mandeville espoused was his vigorous defence of luxury.[128] One modern scholar has said:

'Mandeville's ingenious apology for luxury ... fired the opening gun for the controversy on the subject which waged through the century.'[129]

Mandeville himself wanted to refute the:

'receiv'd Notion, that Luxury is as destructive to the Wealth of the Whole Body Politic, as it is to that of every individual Person who is guilty of it ...'[130]

The use of the word 'guilty' signifies the extent to which Mandeville's contempories considered the very notion of luxury as in some way sinful. Even a writer like Fenelon, who had appreciated the part luxury might play in promoting national wealth, condemned it on moral grounds.[131] Mandeville chooses a rigorous definition of luxury,[132] counting it to be all 'that is not immediately necessary to make Man subsist as he is a living Creature.'[133] He then considers, without resorting to the full rigour of his definition, 'luxury goods' imported from Turkey to see whether they tend to be 'destructive to the wealth of the Whole Body Politic.'[134] His argument is a mercantilist[135] one, observing that if the English leave off this Turkish trade, it will fall into the hands of rivals such as the Dutch or the French. He concludes that as long as:

'Imports are never allow'd to be superior to the Exports, no Nation can ever be impoverish'd by Foreign Luxury; and they may improve it as much as they please, if they can but in proportion raise the Fund of their own that is to purchase it.'[136]

It is the responsibility of politicians to ensure a proper balance of trade by the imposition of certain duties and the removal of others.[137] An important effect of an increased demand for luxury goods will be on employment. In the 'Grumbling Hive' Mandeville shows how full employment results from the growing expectations of life in expanding, commercial societies. The actual perception of luxury changes continually:

'So that many things once look'd upon as the Invention of Luxury, are now allow'd even to those that are so miserably poor as to become the Objects of publick Charity, may counted so necessary, that we think no Human Creature ought want them.'[138]

In the <u>Fable</u> itself Mandeville describes the wide range of activities which were required for the production of a piece of crimson cloth, cited as a possible inspiration for Adam Smith and as a presage to Mandeville's own enunciation of the division of labour in Part II of the <u>Fable</u>.[139] He exclaims on the subject of the crimson cloth:

'But to what Height of Luxury must a Nation be arrived, where not only the King's Officers, but likewise his Guards, even the private Soldiers should have such impudent Desires.'[140]

But Mandeville defends luxury on more than just economic grounds. He attacks the moralists' suspicion of it, denying that luxury has an inervating effect or leads to effeminacy.[141] That would only be the case if individuals indulged themselves to excess. Moreover only a small minority of citizens, members of the 'beau monde', would have access to much luxury. For the vast majority, from whome the ranks of the army were drawn, opportunities would be very limited. The security of the state was not under threat. In fact Mandeville went further, arguing that the promotion of luxury, far from damaging states, was inextricably bound up with their greatness. The full impact of Mandeville's heterodoxy[142] is difficult for us to appreciate but we need to remember that luxury had been deprecated since early Christian times.[143] While S Jenyns supported Mandeville's enthusiastic defence of luxury,[144] other 'Moderns', like Defoe could not entirely ignore the ancient connotations. Writers less committed to the defence of trade, railed openly against those 'who too much indulge the luxury of life, and are too busy with the vain diversion of a wicked age ...'[145]

In <u>Alciphron</u>, partly levelled directly against Mandeville, Berkeley dwelt upon the collapse of Ancient Rome, ascribing luxury and abundant wealth as causes of it.[146]

Mandeville's polemical advocacy of luxury eventually led Hume, in <u>Of Refinement in the Arts</u>, to attempt to steer a course between

'the position of the 'men of severe morals' who regarded even "innocent" or the most moderate luxury as the root of evil, and ... the ... "Libertine view" which saw even the most excessive forms of luxury as a social blessing.'[147]

Hume distinguished between "innocent" and "vicious" luxury, judging the former to be harmless refinement in 'the arts and conveniences of life', positively beneficial to the growth and development of nations.[148] 'Vicious' luxury was quite another matter, for any beneficial effects there might be, were only enjoyed by the individual at the expense of society at large. Hume also attacked Mandeville's assertion that luxury led to full employment, arguing:

'To say, that, without a vicious luxury, (the) labour would not have been employed at all, is only to say, that there is some other defect in human nature, such as indolence, selfishness, inattention to others, for which luxury, in some measure, provides a remedy; as one poison may be an antidote to another. But virtue, like wholesome food, is better than poisons, however corrected.'[149]

Hume has surely fallen into Mandeville's hands here, for the doctor would have retorted: 'But, indeed Sir, Virtue is better than poisons, 'tis a pity we live in a world where disagreeable medicines must be administer'd and where, as you must allow, men can only be moved from their natural state of sloth and stupidity by stirring their passions and, by dextrous management, rousing them to action.'

Hume himself seemed to recognize the weakness of his own position and the truth of Mandeville's assertions about human nature. Summarising his own argument he says:

'Luxury, when excessive, is the source of many ills; but it is in general preferable to sloth and idleness, which would commonly succeed in its place, and are more hurtful both to private persons and to the public.'[150]

Mandeville's advocacy of luxury is therefore closely linked to his psychological observations about human nature. The desire for luxury is an expression of the passion of avarice. By stressing the social importance of promoting luxury, Mandeville propounds his polemical theory that society is possible because of the 'vices' of men. The psychological, rather than the economic, significance of his argument is most important.

Mandeville's defence of luxury earned him notoriety and associated him with commercialism and the morality of the market. Not only did this mean that he was attacked by outraged clerics, but also it meant that he was subject to the vicious ill-humour of those of the 'Bolingbroke circle', like Swift, Pope and Gay who associated economic doctrines with Walpole and 'Robinocracy.'

A comparison between Mandeville and Swift is especially interesting. Both satirized the society of their day. Swift, as much as Mandeville, was concerned to 'show the incompatibility between traditional moral standards and actual ways of living.'[151] Their satire had roots in both the English tradition of Sam Butler in 'Hudibras'[152] and in the continental <u>moraliste</u> literature of writers like La Rochefoucauld.[153] But there is an important difference in the satire of Mandeville and Swift, namely that unlike Mandeville, Swift could not accept the 'great hive', indeed he deplored the development of the kind of society where luxury and abundance became the order of the day. Swift totally rejected the values of commercialism and he did not accept Mandeville's propostion that a nation must be 'vicious' to be 'great'. Swift dedicated a good deal of energy to attacking that avarice which he saw as the basis of the new Walpole whiggery: in Gulliver's Travels the obsession with money is part of Yahoo moral corruption. In the Modest Proposal, which has been suggested may have been a direct retort to Mandeville, Swift exposes the malpractices of the English government in Ireland and recommends cannibalism as a solution to the problem of poverty in that land, thereby cruelly parodying the principle of private vices, public benefits.[154]

Pope and Gay were part of the literary opposition to Walpole's regine. Pope had included Mandeville in his vast compendium of scorn and contempt, the Dunciad,[155] but it is in the Epistle to Bathurst[156] that he attacks Mandeville's notion that luxury is bound up with national greatness. The reverse, Pope says, is true. He draws a graphic picture of the paralysing effects of luxury in these lines:

>'At length Corruption, like a gen'ral flood
>(So long by watchful Ministers withstood)
>Shall deluge all; and Av'rice creeping on,
>Spread like a low-born mist, and blot the Sun;
>Statesman and Patriot ply alike the stocks,
>Peeress and Butler share alike the Box,
>And Judges job, and Bishops bite the town,
>And mighty Dukes pack cards for half a crown.
>See Britain sunk in lucre's sordid charms,
>and France reveng'd of ANNE's and EDWARD's arms!'[157]

The theme of decline is taken up by Gay whose Beggar's
Opera,[158] is an extended parody of the new 'moneyed' society. Gay
takes the rather Mandevillean view of the world as a great stage of
cheats where only the pomposity of people like statesmen and
priests really distinguish them from the underworld of beggars and
thieves.[159] However, this is meant to be a satire on the decadence
of the times and not, as implied by Mandeville, a description of
how things must always be. In his tenth political Fable,[160] Gay
takes up Mandeville's actual imagery from the 'Grumbling Hive',
reversing it to show how ruin and disaster follow the introduction
of vice into a hive of bees.[161]

These 'debates' about luxury and corruption may be seen in the
wider context of the great seventeenth and eighteenth century
dialogue between the 'Ancients' and the 'Moderns; by this time
metamorphosized, in a characteristically Augustan manner, into a
discussion about the relative merits of ancient and modern
societies. The seventeenth century debate in France had
concentrated on the matter of the superiority of classical over
modern literature. In England Godman and Hakewell, Stubbe and
Glanvill, Temple and Wooton, to name some of the leading
protagonists, turned the debate into a philosophical and
scientific, as much as a literary confrontation.[162] Bacon was the
champion of the 'Moderns' who rejected dogmatic Aristotelianism.[163]
These English men of science, institutionally organised after 1660
in the Royal Society, enthusiastically extolled the modern advances
that had resulted from the 'experimental philosophy'. Stubbe, a
champion of the 'Ancients', claimed that their aim was to

'supplant a humanist education based upon the classics with a
material and mechanical education.'[164]

Mandeville, himself a man of scientific education,[165] was
committed to empirical methods which Locke had popularized and

which had become accepted by the 'Moderns'. He was also influenced
by the mechanical philosphy of Hobbes. Within the specific context
of the debate about luxury and commercialism, the 'Moderns'
welcomed the growth of luxury trade; whilst the 'Ancients' deplored
it and like Bolingbroke, harked back to a period of republican
virtue, modelled upon early Roman history. Critics of the 'Modern'
analysis concentrated on exposing the dangers of a doctrine that
substantially damaged the notion of free-will by its implied
determinism. Swift, in particular, recognized the moral
implication of the new science. A modern scholar has given a
succinct account of the importance of the concept of free will in
several of Swift's works of this period:

'Since man's will is conceived of as free, a constant threat
to his humanity is a deterministic or mechanistic conception of
motive which would persuade him that his power to choose is in any
way circumscribed. Hence Swift's moral satire on numerology and
deterministic Calvinism in a Tale of the Tub, on astrology in the
Partridge-Bickerstaff papers, on quantitative social science in the
Modest Proposal; and on the theory of unpremeditated, natural
literary inspiration in the Battle of the Books.'[166]

Determinism is a matter we shall consider in the context of
Mandeville's psychology in the next chapter but its association
with the 'new philosophy' is worth noting.

As a 'Modern', Mandeville shared the optimism of those who
throughout the eighteenth and nineteenth centuries espoused the
cause of 'progress'. His optimism was not, however, of a radical
or utopian kind but consisted of a practical recognition of the
achievements of his own civilization.[167] From the dismal
conditions of primitive life, man had achieved a certain level of
material living, evidenced in the 'refinements' of an age as
'polite' as the Augustan one.[168] Progress had been achieved over a
vast time span; evolution was a slow process during which man had

learnt to adapt to the sometimes savage conditions of his
environment. Starting as a fearful and pathetic creature, man's
instinct leads him to seek, by way of the family, the benefits of
social arrangements. In society he finds a possibility for
satisfying the 'multiplicity of his desires'.[169] A reciprocity of
needs and services provides, providentially, a basis for social
arrangements although these will have to be 'skilfully managed' by
politicians and lawgivers.[170] The 'skilful management' of
politicians consists in their ability to regulate men's passions
and thereby allow the 'natural harmony',[171] which providentially
arises from conflicting interests, to evolve. It is a task that
cannot always be carried out to the fullest satisfaction of
leaders: unforeseen factors constantly throw the best plans off
course.

Mandeville understands politics as a process of exercising
psychological skill.[172] He falls short of the rational optimism[173]
of the Enlightenment in believing in the ability, or at least
potential men can have, to predict and therefore to control, their
own destiny. He shares Adam Ferguson's and Adam Smith's
recognition of the complexity of social organisation and the
impossibility of complete control of human affairs. Substituting
the notion of Providence or collected wisdom for God, he would have
agreed with Smith that:

'We tend to exaggerate greatly the extent and the role of the
human, conscious or deliberate purposes, foresight and planning
involved, or to impute to the wisdom of men much of what is in fact
more largely due to the wisdom of God, the designer of the
psychological and social mechanism which makes men in much of their
behaviour unconscious servants of their common welfare.[174]

Such a view implies that it is best to allow the natural
process of the harmony of interests to develop spontaneously,
without the impediment of strict controls. That 'harmony' results
as much from chance as design. In Schatz' words:

'L'harmonie ... existe entre les interets individuels,
harmonie objective et non plus subjective, tenant non pas à un
penchant naturel à la sociabilite, non pas à une intention de ceux
qui la realisent, mais tenant, à l'enchainment involontaire des
nous rapports economique.'[175]

In advanced, 'polite' societies the 'enchainment involontaire'
will be characterized by a division of labour, allowing the
necessary specialization for the production of a sophisticated
range of goods and services. Other aspects of social life will
depend upon an artificial identification of interests;[176] these
being the policies and strategies implemented by lawgivers,
moralists and politicians. Their task is to ensure the smooth-
running of the social mechanism[177] by harnessing men's passions
toward serving society as a whole. In the context of his own
society, Mandeville urged that certain policies should be pursued
which best accorded with this objective: the encouragement of trade
and of luxury, tempered by the mercantilist condition of a balance
of trade in each sector. It was also necessary to ensure a
harmonious legal and political framework, which the 'balanced
Constitution' of Britain luckily provided.

Mandeville's account of social evolution, of socialization and
his political and economic doctrine are processes in the
psychological conditioning of the individual members of society so
as to contribute to the harmonious functioning of the whole. Some
of the processes, for example, social evolution, are 'natural',
that is, they come about as the result of many 'favourable
accidents,'[178] they are not man-made or designed. Other aspects
require more active participation - thus the skills of 'skilful
politicians'[179] are necessary to help create a sense of public

interest, or to turn 'private vices' in to 'public benefits'. But their art must be entirely built 'upon the Knowledge of human nature.'[180] It is time to examine more closely the psychological theory that underlies all Mandeville's social thought.

CHAPTER III: PSYCHOLOGICAL EGOISM

Most modern critics of Mandeville, alluding to his egoism, associate him with Hobbes.[1] In this matter they follow contemporary opinion since many clerics saw Mandeville as a latter-day Hobbist who had not a trace of any God-fearing sense. There has been little attempt to examine the intricacies of Mandeville's psychology, which is advanced and sophisticated for his time, and which, I argue throughout this book, is at the centre of his system of thought.[2]

I shall begin my analysis of his psychology by considering those of his explanations which are causal ones. In his causal theory of human behaviour we find two types of proposition: straightforward generalizations about the physical state of men while they are influenced by particular passions, which are descriptive, and psychological generalizations about habitual or unconscious behaviour, which are explanatory.

The descriptive generalizations are themselves of different sorts. The simpler ones describe the 'symptoms' which may be observed in men who are under the influence of a passion. As the following passage setting out the physical effects of shame shows, they can be graphically clinical:

'When a Man is overwhelm'd by Shame, he observes a sinking of the Spirits; the Heart feels cold and condensed, and the blood flies from it to the Circumference of the body; the face glows, the Neck and part of the Breast partake of the fire, He is heavy as Lead, the Head is hung down, and the Eyes, through a mist of confusion are fixed on the ground ...'[3]

Mandeville's close observation of physical symptoms reminds us of his medical background.[4] His words are clinical and describe what is happening to a man in the medical terminology of his time. By contrast with the symptoms of a shame-ridden man, in a proud one:

'His Spirits swell and fan the Arterial Blood, a more than ordinary warmth strengthens and dilates the heart, the Extremities are cool, he feels light to himself, and imagines he would tread on Air, his Head is held up, his Eyes roll'd about with sprightliness ...'[5]

More complex descriptions of a causal sort relate to the physiology of men of particular 'humours', sometimes implying a necessary connection between a particular physiological state and a passionate one. Thus in 'Remark R', when discussing courage, Mandeville says:

'I shall prove, that ... what the greatest Heroe differs in from the rankest Coward, is altogether Corporeal, and depends upon the inward make of Man. What I mean is called Constitution; by which is understood the orderly or disorderly mixture of Fluids in our Body; that Constitution which favours Courage, consists in the Natural Strength, Elasticity, and due Contexture of the finer Spirits, and upon them wholly depends what we call Stedfastness, Resolution and Obstinancy.'[6]

In that passage Mandeville most nearly approaches a vulgar theory of determinism, postulating a necessary connection between the physiological make-up of an individual and his psychological reactions. However, even here, at his crudest level of analysis, Mandeville does not ignore the fact that the circumstances in which a man finds himself will influence his behaviour on particular occasions.[7] He owes this refinement to his having subscribed to sensationalist psychology of Locke,[8] according to whom external stimuli are the forces that move men to action, and as these vary, so will the behaviour of individuals vary, regardless of their 'constitution' being the same.

However these physiological descriptions are only part of
Mandeville's causal system. When Mandeville speaks of the 'natural
Causes,'that oblige them (men) to act as they do',he is referring
to the 'passions' which move men to act when they perform that vast
area of habitual and 'unthought of' action which constitutes daily
living. The analysis he undertakes in these cases is psychological
- in other words he searches out the operation of the 'passions' in
the behaviour of men and he does not, in any sustained way, attempt
to relate them to the 'constitution' of men. The passions are
themselves, at this level of analysis, the first 'causes' and their
operation is offered as an explanation of different kinds of human
behaviour. Any physiological description he might add is
supplementary to this mechanical account of the passions as causes
which move men to action.

Sometimes in this kind of analysis, Mandeville considers the
mechanical operation of the passions in general terms. Thus he
explains the behaviour of mothers toward children, in terms of the
mother's passion of self-liking, which she is not necessarily aware
of. The children themselves, when playing with animals, will try
to impose their will upon them, in this case being 'moved' by the
'love of Dominion and that Usurping Temper all Mankind are born
with.'[8] In that way a 'category' of behaviour is explained in
terms of a passion as its 'cause'.

Another method of Mandeville's exposition of the passions-as-
causes is to construct a hypothetical individual, examine his
behaviour and then reveal the 'causes' which direct it, but which
the agent himself may not know about. In a Dialogue in Part II of
the Fable,[9] Horatio and Cleomenes discuss the behaviour of an
elegant man of the world, endowed with great wealth, who
nevertheless leads an exemplary life of modesty and restraint.
This member of the 'beau monde' may be convinced that he acts from
consciously selected principles; in fact the real 'cause' of his
behaviour is 'an excessive thirst after praise, and an immoderate
desire of general applause.'[10]

The same method of analysis is found in his other works. In
Free Thoughts, the life history of certain hypothetical characters
is examined and in each case the underlying cause of their
behaviour is exposed.[11] In these 'case-histories', Mandeville
attempts to consider the operation of the passions in sets of
particular circumstances, rather than just in a generalized pattern
of behaviour like the maternal or infantile behaviour we have
already considered. Sometimes he concentrates on a general pattern
of behaviour in particular circumstances. So he takes the case of
a miser and an extravagant man, generalized types, confronted with
a decision as to whether or not to smash an expensive glass, the
particular circumstances. Despite the fact that the miser appeared
to have a free choice in the matter, feeling that he had a 'power
... to determine his Judgement either way',[12] he was restrained to
the point of being unable to act, while the other man, broke the
glass without hesitation. In both cases:

'Each was prompted to do what he did, and overruled by a
predominant passion.'[13]

The passions thus govern men, even 'unknown to themselves',[14]
and in this part of his mechanico-causal theory, Mandeville has
become deterministic.[15] Human behaviour has been interpreted as an
irrational and mechanical response to the sway of instincts.

Before considering the extent of Mandeville's determinism, I
would like to stress that I have so far been concerned only with
certain of his generalizations about human behaviour, namely those
where he portrays man as a machine, propelled by his passions.
These are descriptions of the physiological state of man, under the
influence of particular passions, sometimes implying a connection
between physical states and psychological characteristics; or
psychological generalizations about the causes of a general pattern
of behaviour, sometimes in a particular set of circumstances. In
the latter case

that behaviour is explained by revealing the antecedent states of emotion, the passions, which initiate them. Satisfaction of the passions by behaving in accordance with their prompting, leads to pleasure. The desire for pleasure will again prompt men to certain behaviour. Mandeville's psychology, in its mechanical form, is thus Hobbist, portraying man as an appetitive machine, moved by his passions towards what pleases him, and possessing an inbuilt system of desires which are causally related to what benefits his motion.[16] In this system, 'self-liking' is the 'predominant passion', but avarice, fear, anger, lust and love, envy and jealousy may also act as first causes. Men do not recognize the passions as the causes of their behaviour - indeed that mechanism which I have termed 'cognitive derangement'[17] makes the process of introspection a painful one and leaves men with the belief that they make free choices, whereas in fact:

'All human creatures are sway'd and wholly governed by their Passions, whatever fine Notions (they) may flatter (them) Selves with ...'[18]

The causal generalizations which I have so far considered are generalizations about the behaviour of man in civil society. They seek to explain the behaviour of the individual human machine within the context of social environment. But the social context also implies purposive behaviour on the part of men: their joining together to achieve certain ends. This leads us to Mandeville's theory of motivation.

That Mandeville concerns himself with purposive action which men undertake to achieve certain ends is made clear in a passage where Horatio and Cleomenes are discussing whether one should put a favourable or unfavourable construction upon the motives for men's behaviour in circumstances which afford a choice of interpretation. Cleomenes says:

'The most favourable Construction with all my Heart: But what is that to the Purpose, when all the straining in the World cannot make it a good one? I don't mean the Thing itself, but the Principle it came from, the inward Motive of the Mind that put him upon the performing of it, for it is that in a free Agent, which I call the Action: And therefore call it what you please, and judge as charitably as you can, what can you say of it?'[19]

In this example Mandeville understands 'action as involving an agent's premeditation. This is different from the 'operation of the passions' in the cases I have been considering so far, since in them, the agent is unaware of the causes of his behaviour.[20] Mandeville has entered new psychological territory, that of human motivation. Even so these 'motives' which appeal to men's consciousness are, of course, related to the passions, most importantly to the instinct to seek the approbation of fellow-man, a feature of 'self-liking'. Thus he says:

'To define the Reward of Glory in the amplest manner, the most that can be said of it, is, that it consists in the superlative Felicity which a Man, who is conscious of having performed a noble Action, enjoys Self-Love, whilst he is thinking on the Applause he expects of others.'[21]

The 'applause a man expects of others' is, by corollary a motive for future action - action in the sense of premeditated, purposive behaviour. In civil society, this action may be recognised in distinctive patterns of behaviour, for example, in the pattern of actions of 'men of honour'.'[22]

Men of honour self-consciously seek to distinguish themselves[23] which they must do, of course, within the framework of the conventions[24] governing 'honourable behaviour' in their society. Honour arises from the passion of self-liking, which may be 'observed in Infants, as soon as they begin to be <u>conscious</u> and to <u>reflect</u>.'[25] Consciousness and reflection lead men to consider what they do in the light of others' opinions of themselves.

Mandeville explains it in this way:

'When A performs an Action which, in the eyes of B, is laudable, B wishes well to A; and to show his Satisfaction, he tells him, that such an Action is an Honour to Him, or that he ought to be Honoured for it: By saying this, B, who knows that all Men are affected with Self-Liking, intends to acquaint A, that he thinks him in the right to gratify and indulge himself in the Passion of Self-Liking. In this Sense the Word Honour, whether it is used as a Noun or a Verb, is always a Compliment we make to Those who act, have or are what we approve of; it is a Term of Art to express our Concurrence with Others, our Agreement with them in their Sentiments concerning the Esteem and Value they have for themselves.'[26]

In this explanation of 'honourable' behaviour, Mandeville is concerned with the actions of individuals conscious of their behaviour[27] and capable of responding to actions of their fellow men. 'Honourable' actions are thus actions societally approved. They will be deliberately undertaken by individuals to gain social approval which itself satisfies their passion of self-liking. Mandeville's motivational theory is thus egoistic, linking the conscious, purposive striving of men, to the satisfaction of their passions. 'Men of honour' accord their behaviour to certain rules for the accomplishment of ends they seek.

Mandeville considers other types of behaviour in terms of the purposive model. His mercantilist leanings led him to consider the activity of men engaged in buying and selling. Here the motivation is avarice, the desire for wealth, and it is recognized and consciously acted upon by men who are deterimed to make profits.[28] No one engaged in trade can be unaware of this kind of motivation.

However, the most important social activity of a purposive nature is that of politics where the supreme aim of politicians is, by 'dextrous management', to turn 'private vices' into 'public benefits'. Politicians have to recognize man's passionate nature, They have:

'two main Points to consider, at setting out; first what things will procure Happiness to the Society under their Care; secondly, what Passions and Properties there are in Man's Nature, that may either promote or obstruct this Happiness.'[29]

Politicians[30] themselves, in Mandeville's account, are motivated by a conscious purpose - that is the happiness of the society under their care. But lest this seems too benign, Mandeville does emphasize that personal satisfaction is gained in that pursuit. Like other men, politicians act to please themselves and predominately to satisfy the instinct to be thought pre-eminent, to be glorified, which arises from self-liking.[31]

Mandeville's theory of political motivation, like his general theory of motivation, is hedonistic and egoistic. He tells us, with a flourish:

'Man is never better pleas'd then when he is employ'd in procuring Ease and Pleasure, in thinking on his own Worth, and mending his Condition upon Earth. Whether this is laid on the Devil or our Attachment to the World, it is plain to me, that it flows from Man's Nature, always to mind to Flatter, Love, and take Delight in himself; and that he cares as little as possible ever to be interrupted in this grand Employment.'[32]

The 'grand employment' of pursuing ones pleasures and acting in one's own interest is always the object of deliberative, purposive action. This is not a late theme in Mandeville, for in his early essays, the <u>Female Tatlers</u>, he had already discussed the thirst men have for praise and their displeasure at action which seems of no benefit to themselves.[33] In society, to make

themselves more agreeable to others, men have to learn a subtle
conceit, namely to pretend not to be concerned with their own
interest so that way their actions become more acceptable to
others. Such critical self-examination is a difficult undertaking
but

'if the most publick spirited man will be pleased strictly to
examine himself, he will find that he has never committed any
action deliberately but for its own sake; for he had a satisfaction
either in the doing of it or in the hopes of praise, which sooner
or later he would receive for it.'[34]

Mandeville thus postulates that men always act deliberatively
in order to satisfy their desires. Usually the satisfaction of
these desires is directly linked to the satisfaction of the passion
of self-liking. Indeed there are times, as the following passage
shows, when Mandeville speaks of his 'predominant passion' as if it
is exclusive:

'When this Self-liking is excessive, and so openly shown as to
give Offence to others, I know very well it is counted a Vice and
call'd Pride: But when it is kept out of Sight, or is well
disguis'd as not to appear in its own Colours, it has no Name, tho'
Men act from that and no other Principle.'[35]

Mandeville's motivational theory is thus thoroughly egoistic
because he maintains that men can only be motivated in their own
self-interest. It is subtle enough, however, to be able to account
for action which they take on behalf of others or in accordance
with the dictates of their own 'moral instinct'. Because men
desire the praise and the applause of other men, they will act to
achieve it even in cases where they have to put aside their own
apparent interest. This explains why men of honour will risk their
lives to live up to a code. But every action they undertake is
calculated to raise applause and gratifies the enormous good-will
such men bear to themselves. The social importance of the

instinct to seek the approbation of other men can hardly be over-emphasized. Mandeville says we are possessed of no other quality so beneficial to society.[36]

Mandeville thus concerns himself with explanations which give a causal account of the relationship between men's behaviour and the passions which guide men to this behaviour and also with explanations about men's motives in the special sense of these motives being purposes for their undertaking certain kinds of action. These explanations are not differentiated by Mandeville himself - indeed in his exposition they are inextricably bound with each other and he moves from the mechanical model to the rule-following model freely and sometimes within the course of describing a particular pattern of behaviour. Moreover, whether concerned with explanations in terms of his mechanical or rule-following model, Mandeville understands the 'passions' as the crucial factor in explaining human activity. They are:

'the very Powers that govern the whole Machine, and, whether they are perceived or not, determine or rather create the Will that immediately precedes every deliberative action.'[37]

'Wilful' behaviour is therefore, according to Mandeville, as much the result of the passions as behaviour which is unreflective and which we have seen, he explains causally in terms of a mechanical theory. Moreover, by making the 'will' depend upon the desires of men in the Hobbist manner,[38] he ensures that his motivational theory, that is his theory about 'voluntary' acts, is both egoistic and hedonistic. It is egoistic because the motives which lead men to particular action arise from their self-regarding desires, particularly the desire to gain applause, and it is hedonistic because the object of fulfilment of the will is pleasure, the satisfaction of desire.[39]

Mandeville's treatment of the will and his admixture of causal and motivational explanation is particularly well-illustrated in an interesting part of the <u>Free Thoughts</u>. It occurs in a section on free will and predestination, which begins with Mandeville following Hobbes,[40] in regarding the will as properly the last result of deliberation immediately preceding action. He goes onto consider why it appears to men that their action is free or voluntary, saying that it is

'because we are Conscious, that in the choice of Things we feel a Power (which we perceive not to be controlled by anything) to determine our Judgement either way.'[41]

Nevertheless, despite this feeling of being able to influence our choice, we find that we are compelled to choose one action rather than another - the will has been 'determined' or 'created' by the passions.[42] The 'appetites and inclinations' indeed 'seduce' the will. Mandeville illustrates his theory by taking the case of a miser confronted with the challenge of breaking an expensive glass. Although it appears to the miser that he has a choice as to whether he smashes the glass or not, no psychologist will doubt for a moment that he cannot but be prompted by his overwhelming instinct to preserve it. The possibility of choice in such a case is an illusion: the passions operate as uncontrollable 'causes' of action.

Mandeville adds a further, clinical observation on the operating of different passions-as-causes. He says that:

'we may sometimes observe one part of the Body yet employed in executing a former Will, whilst another shall be already obeying the Commands of the latter: but when we act slowly, and what is called deliberatively, the Motives of very Volition must be obvious to all that have the Courage, as well as Capacity, to search into them.'[44]

Self-knowledge is a possibility but it requires a man of severe disposition to undertake that examination of his own motives that will lead to it.

This section of Free Thoughts reveals Mandeville's concern with various types of explanation - causal-mechanical explanation for unreflective, habitual behaviour accompanied by physiological description; and explanation of motivated 'action', that is, of reflective behaviour of which the agent is aware. This mixture reflects the possibility of offering explanation of behaviour at different 'levels'. It is a pattern to 'be' found in all his writing. Thus in 'Remark R' of the Fable,[45] he shows that it is possible to explain 'honourable' men's action in terms they themselves would accept (ie. of motivation) and simultaneously to explain[46] it in terms of a fixed, human constitution.[47] The latter type of explanation does not concern motives and is part of his mechanico-causal theory.

Similarly, in the Origin of Honour we find Mandeville giving 'mixed' explanations. On the one hand he is concerned with a description of the physiological state of a man under the influence of a particular passion and talks of the 'mechanism of man'.[48] On the other hand, he concerns himself with deliberative behaviour. The following passage shows is an example of the second:

'When a Man wavers in his Choice, between present Enjoyments of Ease and Pleasure, and the Discharge of Duties that are troublesome, he weighs what Damage or Benefit will accrue to him upon the Whole, as well as from the Neglect as the Observance of the Duties that are prescrib'd to him; and the greater the Punishment is he fears from the Neglect, and the more transcendent the Reward is which he hopes for from the Observance, the more reasonably he acts, when he sides with this Duty.'[49]

Mandeville thus recognizes a difference between behaviour which is unreflective and that which is purposive and he offers different explanations for them - the former he explains causally by way of a mechanical theory of the passions; the latter he explains in terms of motives which sitr people to act.[50] However, both types of explanation depend upon a single source - namely the passions and particularly the passions of self-love and self-liking.[51] In Mandeville's mechanico-causal explanations, pride operates as a moving force which propels men toward the objects which please them and away from the objects which displease them, in the Hobbist manner.[52] As self-love is the main source of human energy, his theory is egocentric. In his motivational theory, it is the thought of the applause a man will receive by undertaking certain actions which motivates him and this motivation arises because self-liking is assauged by such applause. As self-liking is the general ground of human motivation, his motivational theory is egocentric. Self-love and self-liking are thus the sources of habitual and reflective behaviour - and both are part of the same self-regarding passion.

We have already seen how Mandeville refined his concept of self-liking, distinguishing it from self-love, in much the same way that the French writers distinguished 'amour de nous memes' from 'amour propre'.[53] The following passage from Part II of the *Fable*, where Mandeville begins his extensive examination of the origin of society, shows us how the two distinct passions work together:

'Self-love would first make it (ie. man) scrape together everything it wanted for Sustenance, provide against the Injuries of the Air, and do everything to make itself and young Ones secure. Self-liking would make it seek for Opportunities, by Gestures, Looks, and Sounds, to display the Value it has for itself, superior to what it has for others ...'[54]

Both passions thus derive from man's self-regard and lead him to self-interested behaviour. Self-love is the 'cause' of the instinctive behaviour of man engaging in self-preservation whilst self-liking provides the motivational basis for action in a purposive sense. It also leads to actions which benefit people other than the agents, a subject to which I shall return.

Mandeville's explanations for different types of human behaviour thus vary and he gives recognition to their differences by distinguishing their origin in self-love and self-liking. However, whilst his mechanico-causal theory is egocentric, having at its centre the self-regarding, appetitive machine, man; his motivational theory is egoistic, postulating self-conscious and self-interested action on the part of reflective agents. Both can be understood against the background of what Leslie Stephen called a 'base view'[55] of human nature, that is, a view which emphasized man as a creature of passions rather than of reason.

This 'base view' is shared by the sceptics and cynics, whose intellectual mentor in this matter was St Augustine.[56] It contrasts with the more 'dignified'[57] psychology of rationalists and optimists who followed St Thomas Aquinas, and in whose ranks the Cambridge Platonists in the seventeenth century and Berkeley, Butler, Shaftesbury and Hutcheson among Mandeville's contemporaries, may be found. Beneath the 'civilized exterior', Stephen says, the cynics like Mandeville represent man a 'an animal moved by base and ferocious passions',[58] a corrupted being from whom the 'dignified' behaviour of rational beings could only be intermittently expected, if expected at all. Although Stephen's critique of Mandevillean psychology is crude, Mandeville does himself draw a pathetic portrait:

'Nothing is so near to a Man, nor so really and entirely his own, as what he has from Nature; and when that dear Self, for the sake of which he values of despises, loves or hates everything else, comes to be stript and abstracted from all Foreign Acquisitions, human Nature makes a poor Figure; it shews a Nakedness, or at least an Undress, which no Man cares to be seen in.'[59]

Expressions of this sort abound in Mandeville's writings.[60] They support his contention that civilization is a frail achievement that man has created in a hostile and chaotic natural environment. Even so, Mandeille is never pessimistic about the human condition. Although he despises the metaphysical optimism[61] of Shaftesbury, he does not despair. Rather pithily, he tells us that

'The attentive Reader, who perused the foregoing part of this Book, will soon percieve that two Systems cannot be more opposite than his Lordship's and mine. His notions I confess are generous and refined: They are a high Compliment of Inspiring us with the most Noble Sentiments concerning the Dignity of our exalted Nature: What Pity it is that they are not true ...'[62]

Although man is a 'low creature' there is a certain jauntiness in Mandeville's acceptance of his limitations. It is the medical man's calmness in the face of the diseased body, a phenomenom he is 'trained' to accept. He claims to have derived his psychology from examining 'human affairs' - that is from an empirical method of gathering evidence from the behaviour of man in society.[63] In fact, Mandeville's generalizations contain elements of deduction as well as induction - he is descriptive, empirical and deductive at the same time.

This admixture may be seen by considering Mandeville's motivational theory where he tells us, in a dazzling phrase, that his subject is 'anatomizing the invisible Part of Man.'[64] This 'anatomizing' consists of introspection on the part of the analyst (which Cleomenes says is a painful process because it affords no pleasure to the agent)[65] into the typical workings of his own motivation and a deduction of similar workings in other people when their observable action is being examined. The empirical element in the theory is the observation of a large number of 'cases' and 'situations' which is Mandeville's constant preoccupation; the deductive part consists in linking this 'observed' behaviour with motives which we know apply to ourselves and, by inference, to all men.[66]

Mandeville's deductive inferences can be found whenever he postulates generalizations relating observed behaviour to specific passions. The actions of people engaged in fighting are related to the passion of anger.[67] Common experiences, like the exposure to weather, can be related to the passion of fear.[68] These types of explanation belong to his mechanical theory of human psychology.

Mandeville, like Hobbes,[69] therefore offers a mixture of deductive and empirical generalizations in his psychology and he explains human behaviour both in terms of a mechanico-causal theory of the passions and an egoistic theory of motivation. He believed, like the natural law theorists, that the laws of human nature:

''were to be discovered by observing the nature of things; in the science of man they were to be discovered by observing the nature of man and his achievements.'[70]

The achievements of the natural law theorists was eventually transformed by Hume and other writers of the Scottish Enlightenment to that 'science of man' whose 'only solid foundation', was, 'experience and observation'.[71] Like the other 'late philosophers'[72] whom Hume cited as contributors to this great advance, Mandeville concentrated on examining man as he appeared to behave in society. His analysis is therefore 'empirical' and his gaze is fixed firmly on the earth below any 'heavenly city'.[73] The most heterodox implication of his psychology was that deterministic element we have seen in <u>Free Thoughts</u>. By attacking free-will, Mandeville was making an assault on the citadel of morality: the ability of men to choose between good and evil.

The determinism illustrated in the <u>Origin of Honour</u>

is confirmed elsewhere in his canon. In a dialogue in Part II of
the **Fable**, Cleomenes, talking about the operation of the passion of
love and answering Horatio's assertion that every action is
determined by the will, says rather tartly:

'What signifies that, where there is a Passion that manifestly
sways, and with a strict Hand governs that Will?'[74]

In **Free Thoughts**, considering the question of free-will and
predestination, Mandeville explains that as men we think we are
free:

'because we are conscious, that in the choice of things we
feel a power (which we perceive not to be controlled by anything)
to determine our judgement either way.'[75]

Mandeville thus isolates consciousness of the power to choose
from the ability to choose itself and while he consistently
explains motivated behaviour as behaviour of which the agent is
conscious; he denies that motivated actions result from will
independent of desire or passion. In fact, all human behaviour,
whether conscious or reflex, arises because of appetites and
passions. The difference is that in the case of the former type,
men are aware of the goals towards which their desire for the
approbation of their fellow-men drives them, whilst in the latter
case they blindly follow their instincts. In either case, they are
driven, truly creations of an Augustinian mind, to the 'unavoidable
Necessity of sinning.'[76]

Mandeville's determinism results from his explanatory
principle and he is not immediately concerned with denying men
freedom to choose their course of action.[77] However, he suggests
that what appears to them to be choice is in fact only the illusion
of choice - they are guided to act in certain ways by the passions
within. Even in cases where men act purposively, their action is

guided by the passion of self-liking and their motives form part of the psychological mechanism which propels them to seek the approbation of their fellows. What seems to be voluntary action is described mechanically, a proposition unacceptable by contemporaries of Mandeville like Cheyne who held that:

'whatever acts mechanically, acts constantly and necessarily, and so can never act voluntarily.'[78]

Cheyne and almost all Mandeville's clerical critics remain in the countryside of voluntary actions outside his determinist fortifications because they cannot see any basis for moral action in the absence of the freedom to choose between good and evil.

However, despite his determinism, as Gregoire has said,[79] Mandeville's thought does not become fatalistic. He does not suggest that all human behaviour is predetermined or predestined to unfold in a certain pattern. Indeed, by contrast, he is sensitive to the progress man has made, through his own efforts, in advancing to civilised society. What Mandeville denies is the possibility of men being free creatures in the sense of their being able to act outside the influence of their passions. Determinism is therefore characteristic of his explanatory system but he does not necessarily exclude freedom on a personal level.

Like Mills doctrine of 'philosophical necessity',[80] Mandeville's psychology includes the possibility of predicting the way a person will act, given a knowledge of his character and circumstances, but it does not restrict his consciousness of action. Moreover, in the social context, Mandeville makes it clear human arrangements are complex and variable. History shows that many events result, in Ferguson's words, from accident rather than design.[81] There is therefore nothing predetermined in the course which historical events may take and man has an important role to play in creating his own destiny.

Mandeville's psychology is presented as a generalized account of human behaviour, more or less applicable to man at any age. In this matter, he shares the widespread eighteenth century belief in the uniformity of human nature, succinctly summarized by Hume in these words:

'It is universally acknowledged, that there is a great uniformity among the actions of men, in all nations and ages, and that human nature remains still the same, in its principles and operations. The same motives always produce the same actions: the same events follow from the same course.'[82]

Hume continues by saying that the various passions, such as ambition, avarice and self-love to name a few, 'mixed in various degrees',

'have been from the beginning of the world, and still are, the source of all actions and enterprises, which have ever been observed among mankind.'[83]

Since Mandeville shares this assumption[84] with Hume and other eighteenth century writers, his psychological generalizations are stated as universals though they arise, as he tells us, from observation of the activities of men in a particular society, to wit, Augustan England. I have already shown that, in fact, Mandeville's psychology contains certain assumptions about human nature, summarizable in his having a 'low view' of man, and that he made certain deductions on the basis of a mechanical theory of causation which fitted in with this picture. His psychology was therefore not as strictly empirical as he would have us believe. Nevertheless, since he did seek confirmation for his view from the contemporary behaviour of men, the question arises as to whether his generalizations have the wide applicability he claims for them or whether they are best understood, as C B Macpherson has said is the case for Hobbes, as valid observations of a particular kind of society, namely market society.[85]

We have seen Mandeville's welcome for the developing commercialism of Augustan England, particularly in his defence of luxury. In this sense, Mandeville is enthusiastic for the development of what Macpherson has described as the 'possessive market society' and which he says can already be seen in seventeenth century England.[86] Market society is one in which individuals 'seek rationally to maximize their utilities'.[87] It is a society in which:

'Exchange of commodities through the price-making mechanism of the market permeates the relations between individuals, for in this market all possession, including men's energies, are commodities. In the fundamental matter of getting a living, all individuals are essentially related to each other as possessors of marketable commodities, including their own powers. All must continually offer commodities (in the broadest sense) in the market, in competition with others.'[88]

Macpherson himself accepts the limitation of the concept of possessive market society as an historical description.[89] Nevertheless an hypothesis can be useful if it can point to the direction and limits of a thinker's 'vision'.[90] Although the theory of possessive individualism can help us in interpreting one side of Mandeville's thought, primarily economic, it can obscure the importance of another side, the psychological, which I claim is central to its thought. A consideration of the relationship of Mandeville's social theory to his psychology may highlight the limitations of using a model of Macpherson's sort.

The ''Grumbling Hive' of 1705 is Mandeville's first venture into social commentary. His works[91] before this time consisted of the academic Latin treatises of his school and university days and the almost purely 'literary' pieces from 1703-1705 when he was

first writing in English. The 'Grumbling Hive', was a jeu
d'esprit, parodying the inconsistency of those who were demanding a
return to the 'simple life' while at the same time enjoying the
benefits of commercial society. It was also, as we shall see in
the next chapter, a juxtapositioning of two moral attitudes which
were inconsistent. However, in the verse ifself, Mandeville as
satirist concentrates on highlighting the inconsistency between
what men preach and what they do. By the time he came to write the
Fable in 1714, Mandeville had embarked upon his life long task of
analysing human behaviour in terms of the passions. It was a quest
he pursued in his later works: in Free Thoughts (1720) he
concentrates on examining the psychology of religion and Part II of
the Fable (1729), he turns his attention to the origin and
evolution of society.

Mandeville's literary career thus begins with the satiric
preoccupations of a moraliste, in the tradition of Rochefoucauld
and French heterodox writers from Montaigne onwards. This means
that his early interest was in a sort of general theorizing about
human nature, admirably suited to one who was also a medical man
and who brought the clinical manner of the doctor to his general
observation of human nature.[92] His interests then develops into a
more thorough-going examination of human behaviour. His work
becomes replete with the kind of theorizing which I have been
considering in this chapter. The early writings tend to be
paradoxical and deliberately showy, the later works are more sober
and analytical. But throughout his works, the interest in
analysing human nature, in developing psychological theory, is
paramount. It takes priority over such diversions as he made into
economic and political theory.

Mandeville's psychological generalizations fall into two main categories: those which explain men's behaviour in terms of causes, the passions that may operate 'unknown' to them; and those which account for conscious or motivated behaviour and are reducible to the passion of self-liking which leads men to seek the approbation of his fellows. Both types of generalization are thus linked to the 'passions' and predominantly to the self-regarding passions of self-love and self-liking. Mandeville calims to have induced his psychology from the empirical evidence, that is, from observing the behaviour of individuals. In fact his mechanical system contains assumptions which he takes for granted and which arise from a secular Augustinianism still haunted by the imagery of man as a fallen and depraved creature. That moral dimension, always lurking under the surface of his clinical detachment, now needs closer attention.

CHAPTER IV: ETHICS

Despite his own protests, Mandeville has traditionally been regarded as an immoral writer, an advocate for vice; as one modern commentator put it:

'he had become (by 1728) a bogeyman, a name with which to frighten the godly and respectable, an author whom one might read in secret to enjoy a paradox, but whom everyone knew to be a moral monster by whose ideas one must not be infected.'[1]

His interest in paradoxes was singled out as a feature of his viciousness and the subtitle of the Fable, 'private vices, public benefits', was regarded as an immoral plea for licentiousness.[2] Mandeville's notoriety was so strongly established that it has affected all subsequent discussion of his ethics. F B Kaye, in his introduction to the authoritative modern edition of the Fable, concentrated on trying to unravel Mandeville's paradox and in doing this, set the paradigm in which modern scholarly discussion of his moral theory has taken place.

Unravelling Mandeville's paradox, 'private vices, public benefits'[3] in fact diverts attention from what is really his major concern in examining ethical phenomena, namely, the provision of a psychology of moral behaviour. It is true that in the early part of the Fable, Mandeville does concern himself with the moralist's task of defining the nature of virtue and vice, insisting on a strictly rigorist standard for judging the morality of actions. But even at this stage,[4] his definitions are given in the context of a psychological analysis of why men behave morally. This psychological explanation of moral behaviour develops into his main interest. We do not therefore find in Mandeville an extensive and prolonged investigation into the abstract questions of the nature of good and evil. Instead we find a sophisticated psychological analysis of how a particular human passion, self-liking, can be the source of moral actions.

Nevertheless, Mandeville begins by considering the nature of good and evil in a formal, philosophical sense. But having abstractly laid out a strictly rigorist standard of virtue, he goes on to show that very few human actions qualify under it. This enables him to eschew substantive ethical questions altogether and instead to examine human actions in terms of his psychological theory of the passions.

Mandeville's early, paradoxical treatment of morality also has to be seen as part of his satirical intention of exposing hypocrisy. He was amused by what he saw as a gap between the professions and practices of his contemporaries. Their hypocrisy arose from their attempt to hold to inconsistent positions, involving a commitment to asceticism and hedonism at the same time. The paradox, 'private vices, public benefits' was the satirical weapon Mandeville used to expose this hypocrisy, to show that what many of his contemporaries held to be pfgreat benefit, namely material wealth, in terms of their professed, ascetic code, would have to arise from private 'vices'.

Most eighteenth century readers of the Fable dwelt on the alleged immorality of Mandeville's paradox, taking his aphorism to be a literal prescription for personal licentiousness.[5] Thus William Law talks of Mandeville's 'compositions in favour of the vices and coruption of mankind'[6] and includes him in the company of those 'sagacious advocates for immorality'.[7] Bluet says the Fable is a 'treatise of impiety',[8] Dennis talks of Mandeville's 'open attack upon the public virtue',[9] Fiddes says that he makes 'no real distinction between virtue and vice',[10] Skelton says that he 'makes vice the spring of everything'[11] whilst Berkeley exposes the fallacy of 'private vice public benefits' by using the example of drunkedness, a private vice of doubtful public benefit.[12] Even Francis Hutcheson, who analyses the various possible meanings of 'private vices, public benefits'[13] concentrates on showing how Mandeville is wrong in associating 'vice' with benefit or prosperity, let alone happiness. At one point he suggests that Mandeville is misusing the word 'vice' arguing, in an utilitarian manner, that if it leads to public benefit, then it cannot be termed 'vice'.[14]

Contemporary reactions to Mandeville arose because of the literalness with which his critics read the phrase 'private vices, public benefits', and because they saw it as a threat to Christian morality. Dennis' view is indicative:

'With whatever design the Fable of the Bees, or Private Vices, Public Benefits, was writ, nothing is more certain, than that it has done, and will do Mischief, by debauching the minds and principles as such of its readers as are not qualified to distinguish right from wrong, and the artifice of sophistry from the justness of reason, which are nineteen parts in twenty of them. It is a treatise that seems as much qualified to encourage vice and luxury, as if it had been contrived on purpose for it, and it is like to insinuate into every person of corrupt manners, who reads it, that the more he is guilty of excess and extravagance in the aforesaid vices, the more he approves himself a good Commonwealth's man, and shows himself a worthy patriot.'[15]

Dennis's words indicate the real concern of Mandeville's contemporaries who answered him or wrote about the Fable, namely that a literal reading of its subtitle or an acquaintance with the book's tone and mood, led one to the opinion that it was a prescription for vice, an apology for what many thought the 'vain diversions of a wicked age.'[16]

Many years after the publication of the first Part of the Fable,[17] Mandeville spoke out on the particular point of the book's subtitle, saying that he had chosen it 'to raise Attention: As it is generally counted to be a Paradox.'[18] He explains that the 'benefits' he referred to were worldly ones (the materialistic values of his own society) whilst the 'vices' were human frailties and passions.[19] His point was that those who maintained these latter human qualities to be 'vicious', refused to accept that they were linked to the worldly benefits they so coveted. They were therefore hypocrites who ignored the clash between their ascetic professions and worldly ambitions.

Mandeville's satirical or <u>moraliste</u> intentions were to satirise the position of such people but his satire was taken by contemporaries to be a prescription for immorality. Subsequently modern scholars have concentrated on the truth or falsity of these allegations of libertinism, largely ignoring his psychology of moral behaviour. As much modern discussion has been influenced by F B Kaye's authoritative introduction to the modern edition of the <u>Fable</u>, we need to consider Kaye's arguments in some depth.[20]

Kaye's exposition of Mandeville's ethics depends upon accepting that there are two different standards being <u>applied</u> by Mandeville in his assessment of the morality of actions: the first is 'rigoristic' (ascetic and rational) and is applied as a criterion for judging the motives of individuals' behaviour; the second is 'utilitarian' and is applied as a criterion for juding the social consequences of such behaviour. For an action to be judged virtuous under the first condition, it must be disinterestedly motivated; that is the individual must be attempting to deny his own inclinations and further he must be doing this because he believes such denial to be good. For an action to be judged virtuous under the second condition, it must result in clear material benefits, or, in other words, be publicly beneficial. By holding to both these standards at the same time, Kaye asserts that Mandeville arrived at his paradox that private vices are public benefits. However, Kaye then says that in fact Mandeville's adoption of the first condition, the 'rigorist' one,

was disingenuous and that by inisting upon the utilitarian
condition at the same time, he was achieving a <u>reductio ad absurdum</u>
of rigorism. And this was entirely understandable since, according
to Kaye, Mandeville's rigorism was cosmetic and had merely been
introduced for satirical purposes.

The confusion in Kaye's treatment of Mandeville's ethics has
been shown up by M J Scott-Taggart.[21] Scott-Taggart is concerned
with rejecting both the traditional view that the <u>Fable</u> was a
testimonial for vice and Kaye's view that the adaptation of two
standards led Mandeville to paradox and to a <u>reductio ad absurdum</u>
of rigorism.[22] In dealing with Kaye's interpretation, Scott-
Taggart says that there may be no inconsistency in holding to the
two standards as Kaye understands them. Scott-Taggart says:

'In a footnote Kaye explains that he is using the terms
'rigorism' and 'utilitarianism' loosely, and intends his use of the
latter term to mark 'an oppostion to the insistence of "rigoristic"
ethics that not results but motivation by right principle
determines virtuousness.'[23]

Where Kaye wrote "The paradox that private vices are public
benefits is merely a statement of the paradoxical mixing of moral
criteria which runs through the book;' Scott-Taggart says that his
meaning is

'The paradox that private vices are public benefits is merely
a statement of the paradoxical mixing of appraisal of conduct in
terms of motive and appraisal of conduct in terms of
consequences.'[24]

But as Scott-Taggart says, the actual 'mixing' itself does not
generate paradox:

'We might analogously be interested both in the dexterity and effectiveness of an action, and discover that, although connected, the two were not exactly correlated with one another. To infer from this that one of them must be dropped as in some way impossible would be absurd; we select between them according to the purposes we want served.[25]

Kaye's interpretation of Mandeville's ethical postion and his allegations that Mandeville achieved a practical <u>reductio ad absurdum</u> of rigorism is therefore based upon misunderstanding.[26] In fact, Mandeville selected, as Scott-Taggart says[27] we might, between appraisal of conduct in terms of motive and appraisal of conduct in terms of consequences, according to his immediate concern. Within the context of his paradox, he was concerned with satirising the position of those people who retained two contradictory ethical criteria, the rigorist and the utilitarian, at one and the same time <u>whether they were appraising conduct in terms of motives or of consequences</u>. It is the contradiction in maintaining the two sets of criteria Mandeville is satirizing; he does not concern himself with the question of appraising in terms of motives or consequences.

Moreover, without minimizing the discovery of Scott-Taggart and others[28] of a logical flaw in Kaye's analysis, particularly important, as I have said, because this analysis has been taken as the starting point for modern, scholarly discussion of the subject; concentration upon unravelling the paradox has diverted attention from what is really important about Mandeville's acount - namely that it is an attempt to explain moral phenomena in terms of human psychology. Mandeville's satirical intentions have attracted the exclusive attention of almost all writers who have considered Mandevillean ethics[29]; yet his satire is only the starting point of his earliest work, the 'Grumbling Hive'. By the time he had written the 'Remarks', Mandeville had developed his ideas about how moral behaviour is generated by the passion of self-liking. To understand this more developed and significant treatment of morality, we must divert our attention from the paradox, private vices, public benefits, to examining the psychological treatment of morality that we find in all Mandeville's works.

It is in the 'Enquiry into the Origin of Moral Virtue', 1714, the essay immediately preceding the prose 'Remarks' which form Part I of the Fable, that we find Mandeville's first full treatment of the subject.[30] As the title implies, Mandeville is concerned with the genesis of morality, a characteristically eighteenth century exercise seeking to explain social phenomena in terms of its origins.[31] The specific literary context of the 'Enquiry' is that of the fable of 'lawgivers and other wisemen that have laboured for the establishment of society.'[32] These men, 'having thoroughly examined' human nature,[33] saw the need to create a myth which would enable the passionate and selfish animals, men, to associate peacefully and profitably together in civil society. This myth took the form of representing men as angelic and rational if they pursued the public good, at the expense of their own interests; and brutish and passionate if they merely pusued their own interest, without regard to any other. The actions of the first group, the 'angelic men', were decreed 'virtuous' since by their self-denial, they benefitted society as a whole; the actions of the latter were deemed 'vicious' since they benefitted no one except themselves. Thus 'virtue' and 'vice' were harnessed toward social ends by making them terms of approbation and disapprobation respectively. In this way 'the first Rudiments of Morality, (were) broach'd by skilful politicians, to render Men useful to each other as well as tractable ...'[34]

In Part II of the Fable, as Mandeville expounds his views of the gradual evolution of society and its institutions over vast epochs, it becomes apparent that the process of 'making' men moral creatures, that is the public consideration of actions as virtuous or vicious in terms of the myth, is, in fact, a long-drawn out and gradual process. The 'invention' of the 'lawgivers' in the 'Enquiry'' must be read allegorically and not literally. It is, as

Lovejoy has said, the device of the satirist.[35] As man becomes a social being by living in society,[36] so too he becomes moral by living in society. Approval for actions deemed publicly beneficial and disapproval of those only privately advantageous is a moral practice that evolves over many ages. Mandeville thus denies that man is naturally a moral being just as he denies that he is naturally a social being - morality and sociability are characteristics only ascribable to 'civilized man', man, that is, who lives in a civil society which is characterized by reciprocal exchange and the enforcement of law.[37]

Against this wider context of an evolutionary social theory we can now examine Mandeville's formal definition of vice and virtue, given in the 'Enquiry'. Man agreed to call any action

'VICE; if in that action there could be observed the least prospect, that it might either be injurious to any of the Society, or ever render himself less serviceable to others: And to give the Name of VIRTUE to every Performance, by which Man, contrary to the impulse of Nature, should endeavour the Benefit of others, or the Conquest of his own Passions out of a Rational Ambition of being good.'[38]

Taking this definition from the point of virtue first, it implies that a virtuous action must involve self-denial (ie. that it is 'contrary to the impulse of nature'), that it must be rational and motivated toward good (ie. that it must be done 'out of a rational ambition of being good') and that it must benefit others (ie. 'the benefit of others') or involve the agent in controlling his instincts (ie. the conquest of his own passions'). The latter two conditions of Mandeville's definition of virtue, namely the 'benefit of others' or 'the conquest of his own passion' represent an utilitarian and ascetic condition respectively. They concern the motives any agent should have for undertaking an action which can qualify for being virtuous. Taken together, these two

conditions for judging actions virtuous, imply contradiction
(indeed the same contradiction as he achieved by juxtapositioning
them in the paradox, 'private vices, public benefits') since an
action done for the 'benefit of others' may not be and may clash
with, an action involving 'the conquest of (one's) own passion.'
However, in Mandeville's definition both these conditions are
qualified by the phrases 'contrary to the impulse of Nature' and
'out of a rational ambition of being good', therefore making the
utilitarian condition only effective for judging the virtuousness
of actions when it is qualified by rational self-denial.
Mandeville's position is made clear if we consider what he said
about pity, namely, that as

'it is an Impulse of Nature, that consults neither the publick
Interest nor our own Reason, it may produce Evil as well as Good.
It has help'd to destroy the Honour of Virgins, and corrupted the
Integrity of Judges; and whoever acts from it as a Principle, what
good soever he may bring to the Society, has nothing to boast of
but that he has indulged a Passion that has happened to be
beneficial to the Publick.'[39]

The fact that the 'indulgence' of pity, has 'happened to be
beneficial to the Publick', that is, that on a strictly utilitarian
condition, it may be deemed virtuous, is not allowed by Mandeville.
Before any action can be regarded as virtuous, it must involve
self-denial from a rational choice of preferring 'good'.[40]

Now this kind of rational and ascetic condition, what Kaye
called 'rigorist', is consistent, in Mandeville's mind, with the
demands of Christian ethics but it is rarely, if ever, to be found
to apply to the actions of men in the world. Human nature, as
Mandeville argues, is passionate; men are governed both in their
conscious and instinctive behaviour by the passions and therfore
the expectation of their behaving in a self-restraining manner is
in Mandeville's view, unrealistic. Really virtuous action, by

which he means action involving at least some element of self-denial, is rare because it is not in keeping with human nature.

Of course there is a further dimension to Mandeville's definition of virtue which I have yet to consider and that is the extent to which, like his infamous paradox, it supports his satirical intentions. That he applied the strict condition of rigorism to support his satire is obvious, but it should be noted that it is the inconsistency of those professing Christianity yet not adhering to an acceptable Christian position, that he satirizes.[41] Thus in <u>Dion</u> he says:

'I have wrote in an Age and a Nation, where the greatest part of the Fashionable, and what we call the better sort of People, seem to be far more delighted with Temporal, than they are with Spiritual Enjoyments, at the same time that they profess themselves to be Christians; and that whatever they may talk, preach or write of a Future State and eternal Felicity, they are all closely attach'd to this wicked World ...'[42]

Inconsistent attitudes are the object of Mandeville's satire and his 'rigorism' is employed to show up the discrepancies between profession and action. Moreover, by adhering to the strict, rigorist position, Mandeville effectively rules out virtuous action altogether since according to rigorist criteria, hardly any actions of men in 'this wicked World'[43] qualify as virtuous.

Has Mandeville eradicated virtue entirely and how can he develop a theory about moral behaviour? The questions arise as a response to what Mandeville says of the behaviour of men in the world when measured agains the strict rigorism which I have been considering. On the rigorist criterion itself, Mandeville has all but excluded the possibility of virtuous actions. This leaves him free to evolve a theory of descriptive ethics which explains what men do when they say they are behaving morally.

The literary myth of the 'lawgivers and other wise men'[44] involved politicians who, having 'thoroughly examin'd' human nature, set out to encourage men to approve of action societally beneficial and disapprove of action entirely self-regarding and without social benefit. It was a device for explaining how men were persuaded to behave morally. It must be emphasized that in this account, such encouragement takes place <u>after</u> human nature has been 'thoroughly examin'd'; in other words, it is action compatible with human nature or the nature of men in the world. When we remove the literary structure of the myth, we are left with Mandeville asserting that it is compatible with the nature of men as they are, to develop a morality by which their actions may be judged. This is not a rigorist morality, nor in expounding it, is Mandeville in fact concerned with any substantive ethical position. What he does intend to explain is moral behaviour within the framework of his psychology.

Mandeville's serious concern in writing about morality is therefore with a psychological account of moral behaviour. His interest is in describing the way in which pursuit of what men think of as 'good' is compatible with their actual nature and dispositions. This compatibility arises from the self-fulfilling potential of moral behaviour. The 'object of Pride' is, he tells us, 'the Opinion of Others'[45] and to none is this opinion more favourably granted, than to those who comply with what is regarded as good in any particular society at any particular time. Men behave morally, that is they pursue what is 'good' in their particular setting because such behaviour leads to the approbation of their fellows and therefore satisfies their self-liking, the predominant human passion. Mandeville does not concern himself with the substantive ethical questions of what good might be, but his psychological theory suggests an extreme relativism which at one point allows him to compare the uncertainty of moral judgement with the uncertainty of taste.[46] It also suggests that moral behaviour is not innate but acquired. For Mandevillean man is no more naturally moral than he is naturally sociable. Notions of right and wrong are acquired

'for if they were as natural, or if they affected us, as early as the Opinion, or rather the Instinct we are born with, of taking everything to be our own, no Child would ever cry for his eldest Brother's Playthings.'[47]

The acquisition of these notions of right and wrong comes through education and is supported by social myth and practice. Children are taught from the earliest age that they can best indulge their passions and particularly the predominant passion of self-liking, by being virtuous, by behaving, that is, in accordance with the acceptable standards of their society. When they have achieved adulthood, as men, they will be buttressed in their 'moral' practices by the flattery that conventional behaviour attracts. Mandeville concludes with an aphorism that attracted considerable notoriety to his name:

'the Moral Virtues are the Political Offspring which Flattery begot upon Pride.'[48]

Men behave morally in order to seek the approbation of their fellows and thereby to satisfy their passion of self-liking. Their appreciation of the applause of their fellows is complex. He argues with some intricacy:

'The Pleasure we receive from Acclamations, is not in the Hearing; but proceeds from the Opinion we form of the Cause, that produces these Sounds, the Approbation of others.'[49]

To gain this applause, 'many virtues ... may be counterfeited'[50] and social intercourse offers many opportunities for men to applaud one another. They may do this with utmost discretion, especially if they be 'Men of tolerable Parts, in plentiful Circumstances, that were artfully educated.'[51] For such men 'can hardly fail of a genteel behaviour'[52] and

'The more Pride they have and the greater Value they set on the Esteem of others, the more they'll make it their Study, to render themselves acceptable to all they converse with; and they'll take uncommon Pains to conceal and stifle in the Bosoms every thing, which their good Sense tells them ought not to be seen or understood.'[53]

In the rare cases where they perform disinterested deeds in silence, men derive a satisfaction from contemplating their own worth; they bask, in such situations, in self applause.[54]

Mandeville therefore stresses the emotive content of moral prescriptions and he subscribes, like Hobbes and Hume, to the view that ethical propostions entail a motivation to act morally,[55] though, as I shall shortly show, this remains within the framework of his egoism. Accordingly, when men understand that an action is good, in the sense that it is societally approved, they are motivated by their instinct to gain praise and they will try to perform the action. When they realize that a certain course of action is bad, that is, that it is disapproved by society, they are deterred from performing it. The performance of moral actions depends upon the stimulation of desires, appetites or passions. Moral action is, of course, purposive action and, as I have considered in the previous chapter, Mandeville does distinguish action of which the agent is aware from mechanical action which involves no consciousness of purpose on the part of the agent. He explains that kind of action causally. However as is the case in his general theory of motivated action, Mandeville's 'approbative' theory of moral action suggests that the pursuit of what is societally regarded as good, may be a semi-automatic process since it involves the stimulation of the passion of self-liking. Human will power is weak and amounts to little more than a consciousness of choice rather than an ability to act upon it.[56]

Thus, for example, men of honour self-consciously pursue the rules of their particular code of behaviour in order to gain the esteem of their fellows and thereby to satisfy their self-liking. They may be aware of the reasons of their own action but, given the nature which they have and given the feebleness of their will to control the impulse of their passions, there seems little scope for them to act against their inclinations. In the same way, because men are fundamentally creatures of their passions and because, ascetically or rigoristically speaking, virtue must consist in the denial of the passions, Mandeville sees little scope for virtuous action understood in this sense. That suits his satirical purpose as well. Furthermore, his specific explanation of moral behaviour, that is, his theory of approbativeness can be shown to be a distinct feature of his egoistic theory, a matter which I shall now consider.

For Mandeville men only act out of self-interest, that is they act to promote their own interest at the expense of the interests of others or they act in their own interest despite the dictates of their conscience. But the self-interest of men consists primarily in satisfying their passions, especially the passion of self-liking, by seeking the approbation of their fellows or by indulging in other-regarding behaviour, that is, behaviour socially approved as virtuous. Thus although men only act out of self-interest, that is they act only to satisfy themselves, this self-interest includes the possibility of actions of benefit to others rather than the agent. Mandeville stresses the social importance of the self-interested passions, for example, in the case of men of honour, whose impulse to seek approbation leads them to risk their lives in the defence of the commonwealth.

Kaye claims that Mandeville's refinement of his notions of self-love and self-liking arose from Butler's criticism of egoistic theories in the *Sermons*, which were delivered between the dates 1714 and 1728, when the respective parts of the *Fable* appeared.[57] In any case the argument between the egoists and altruists had become a major preoccupation of eighteenth century British moralists.[58] It may be said that Mandeville belonged to the Hobbes school of egoists,[59] whilst Shaftesbury and Hutcheson, the latter certainly aware of Mandeville as an opponent to refute, belonged to the Cumberland school of altruists.[60] Of Mandeville's contemporaries, it was Butler who provided the most penetrating criticism of egoistic arguments.

Butler's main argument against the 'reductionist' egoism of Hobbes and Mandeville depends upon criticizing their definition of what is and what is not, selfish. Butler says:

'And if, because every particular affection is a man's own, and the pleasure arising from its gratification on his own pleasure, or pleasure to himself, such particular affection must be called self-love; according to this way of speaking; no creature whatever can possibly act but merely from self-love; and every action and every affection whatever, is to be resolved into this one principle.'[61]

However, he then adds:

'But then this is not the language of mankind; or if it were, we should want words to express the difference between the principle of an action, proceeding from cool consideration that it will be to my own advantage; and an action, suppose of revenge or friendship, by which a man runs upon certain ruin, to do evil or good to another. It is manfest the principles of these actions is totally different, and so want different words to be distinguished by: all that they agree in is, that they both proceed from, and are done to gratify an inclination in man's self. But the principle or inclination is one case self-love; in the other, hatred or love of another.'[62]

Butler's argument amounts to saying that the 'reduction' of all human behaviour to an explanation in terms of a selfish principle is mere tautology since, by definition, all actions of the self must be selfish. Such a definition is a mere truism and has no usefulness in helping us judge of the morality of actions. Indeed, not only is this reduction mere tautology, but it leaves actions of manifestly different sorts undistinguished - it fails to differentiate, that is, between principles of action 'proceeding from cool consideration' of self-advantage from those which run directly counter to the advantage of the agent.

Butler's criticism seems strong when applied to Mandeville's early positon in the first part of the _Fable_ where he has not yet distinguished between self-love and self-liking. At that point Mandeville was simply saying that all actions arise from self-love or pride, although within these actions he included actions of an other-regarding sort. This is unconvincing. Mandeville's early definition was not sharp enough to bear the weight of a 'self-love' which included other-regarding actions, though there is no doubt that he used it in that sense as well as in the more commonly accepted self-regarding sense.

The position changes when Mandeville redefines the passions more carefully in the second part of the _Fable_, a recourse which Kaye hazards is a rejoinder to Butler.[63] In the later definition, whilst self-love is the passion of self-preservation which all men have, self-liking is specifically the instinct to seek the approbation of other man and may dictate actions contrary to the interest of the agent. Mandeville's egoism thus distinguishes action which is merely 'selfish' in the sense that it is an action of the self and action which is 'selfish' in that it is action pleasurable and beneficial to the self but may involve action like Butler's of 'revenge or friendship, by which a man runs upon certain ruin, to do evil or good to another.'[64] This latter action can arise from the passion of self-liking which prompts men to seek the approbation of others. What is more, Mandeville insists that men exclusively act, whether consciously or unreflectively, on the promptings of either self-love or either self-liking. In this way he saves his egoistic theory whilst being able to account for what is judged morally impeccable behaviour even on Butler's standards.

Mandeville thus eludes Butler's criticism that egoism fails to account for actions manifestly different from other actions, that is between actions of benefit to the agent only and those of benefit to other people, for his theory of approbation means that he does explain within the terms of his egoism, how men can act against their own immediate interest. Furthermore, Mandeville's postion is not affected by Butler's argument against Hobbes' treatment of compassion. Butler criticizes Hobbes 'and others who follow in his steps'[65] on the grounds that Hobbes' definition of compassion[66] involves care and imagination of ourselves, whereas, the bishop asserts, compassion must imply an object external to the agent himself towards which his affection is directed. Accordingly, Butler argues, Hobbes' treatment leads to the conclusion that fear and compassion are the same, for the latter is merely a form of fear of the like like consequences of a particular person's situation, happening to ourselves. Butler insists that while fear of a like calamity happening to ourselves may be a consequent reflection after seeing someone in distress and indeed that we may experience a satisfaction 'from our consciousness of our freedom from that misery,'[67] we cannot speak properly of compassion unless there is present a 'real sorrow and concern for the misery of our fellow creatures.'[68]

Mandeville's own definition of compassion avoids the snare of Butler's argument. He says that:

'Pity or Compassion ... consists in a Fellow-feeling and Condolence for the Misfortunes and Calamities of others: all

Mankind are more or less affected with it; but the weakest Minds generally the most. It is raised in us, when the Sufferings and Misery of other Creatures makes so forcible an Impression upon us, as to make us uneasy. It comes in either at the Eye or Ear, or both; and the nearer and more violently the Object of Compasison strikes those Senses, the greater Disturbance it causes in us, often to such a Degree as to occasion great Pain and Anxiety.'[69]

Compassion, then, does involve an object external to the agent himself toward which his affection is directed but, in the direction of that affection, the agent is indulging a passion to his own satisfaction just as he is when, out of the need to satisfy the passion of self-liking, he may engage in activity of no particular advantage to himself but of benefit to somebody else. Compassion therefore, does, for Mandeville, as well as Butler,[70] involve a 'concern for the misery of our fellow creatures,' and a direction of affection toward an object external to the agent. However, for Mandeville it also involves the indulgence of a passion, an activity of self-satisfaction which benefits the agent himself whatever may be its external effects on others.[71]

Butler's critical attacks on the reductionist position thus do not seem to undermine Mandeville's particular version of egoism but the bishop, like Shaftesbury and Hutcheson, went further than a mere rejection of egoism. He, like they, postulated a theory of natural benevolence. Since the three positions viz a viz Mandevillean egoism are not radically different, I shall concentrate on considering Hutcheson's position[72] and suggest that what may be said of his 'moral sense' may be said of Shaftesbury's 'internal sense' or Butler's 'conscience' in the context of this discussion.

For Hutcheson, the argument against egoism partially rests upon a mere assertion of natural human benevolence.[73] He states categorically that men:

'have some instinct antecedent to all reason from interest, which influences (us) to the love of others.'[74] This instinct is the 'moral sense', a refinement of Shaftesbury's[75] 'internal sense' and is implanted in men by 'the author of nature' to motivate them to perform virtuous actions. A joint retort of his and of Shaftesbury's might have been directed specifically at Mandeville:

'The author of nature has much better furnished us for a virtuous conduct, <u>than some moralists seem to imagine</u>, by almost as quick and powerful instincts, as we have for the preservation of our bodies. He has given us strong affections to be the springs of each virtuous action; and made virtue a lovely form, that we might easily distinguish it from its contrary, and be made happy by the pursuit of it.'[76]

The argument is sharpened by Hutcheson when he attacks the hedonistic notion of a desire, saying that desires must have objects which must be logically different from the desires themselves and their gratification. If this were not the case, one could, given an image of pleasure, arouse any desire for the most fantastic objects whereas, according to Hutcheson:

'one cannot have the satisfaction resulting from gratifying a desire unless one really does have and does gratify that desire.'[77]

Desires must therefore have objects which are distinct from them. In the <u>Essay on the Nature of Conduct of the Passions and Affections</u>, Hutcheson says:

'There are in Men Desires of the Happiness of others, when they do not conceive this Happiness as the Means of obtaining any sort of Happiness to themselves. Self-approbation, or Rewards from the Deity, might be the ends, for obtaining which we might possibly desire or will from self-love, to raise in ourselves kind Affections; but we could not from Self-love desire the happiness of others, except we imagined their Happiness to be the means of our own.'[78]

Hutcheson's logical criticism of considering 'desires' in isolation from what it is that an agent desires is a strong point and one of which Mandeville and other hedonists would have to take account. In the case of Mandeville's moral theory, however, the desire which he speaks of is the desire for the approbation of others and is therefore at least as definite an 'object of desire' as Hutcheson's own 'happiness of others.' Indeed, Hutcheson, by arguing in the *Essay* that men have desires for the happiness of others has done little more than make an assertion contrary to the egoistic assertions of Mandeville that this other-regarding 'desire' is always related to self-satisfaction. And his deduction at the end of the passage I have quoted, namely that we could not derive this desire of the happiness of others from self-love unless we considered others' happiness to be the means of our own is exactly what Mandeville does assert to be the case in the operations of the passion of self-liking.

Hutcheson, therefore, like Butler, presented an alternative to an egoistic theory of human nature. He does not conclusively refute it. Like Shaftesbury, and Butler, Hutcheson insisted that man is a sociable creature endowed with an instinct of benevolence which directed him to act in the interests of other men.[79] All three differed from Mandeville in insisting that the satisfaction of the instinct of benevolence was not a 'selfish' act. Looking at it from the other way round, they maintained, against the Mandevillean position, that men were not motivated selfishly (in Mandeville's case, to seek the applause of their fellows), when they pursued courses of action not in their own interest. The strength of Mandeville's position, as he had redefined it when he introduced the distinction between self-love and self-liking, was that he did not deny that men might act in the interests of others; he merely said that when they did so their actions were still 'selfish' and did not arise from natural benevolence.

If Mandeville's 'reduction' of moral behaviour to egoism thus eludes Butler's or Hutcheson's argument, it is at least partly because their own positions are not dissimilar to his. In Hutcheson's case, moral motivation arises from the natural feeling of sympathy which all men have for their fellows, in Butler's it comes from the natural benevolence in them, and in Mandeville it is generated by their self-liking. All three explain moral behaviour in terms of human passions rather than direct attention to the moral demands imposed by duty or divine command. Moreover, intensifying this similarity, both Hutcheson and Butler,[80] accepted that moral actions might, in certain situations, arise from self-love or at least actions arising from self-love may coincide with actions arising from benevolence.

Mandeville's 'reduction' of moral behaviour to egoism was criticized on other grounds by philosophers such as Law and Berkeley who I shall call 'rationalists', and who subscribed to the rigorist ethics Mandeville satirized in his paradox. Their contention was that virtuous actions were performed because men were rational creatures, capable of distinguishing right from wrong and acting accordingly. Thus Law said:

'If therefore Actions only satisfy and content us by being approved by our Reason, it is manifest Proof that our Reason is the principal Agent in our good Actions.'[81]

These Christian moralists appealed to a superior authority, namely that of God who had implanted reason in men and given them the freedom to choose between good and evil. Their objection to Mandeville's treatment of morality was that, in their eyes, it diminished the contrast between good and evil; whilst their objection to his 'low' view of human nature was that it emphasized the passionate nature of man and showed reason and the will, the 'principal agents' of moral actions, to be weak and ineffective. The first of these objections arose as the result of a concentration upon Mandeville's paradox, private vices, public benefits, which as I have already said, I consider to be a mistaken approach. These critics read the aphorism as a blatantly immoral prescription and entirely missed the point of Mandeville's satire. At a weaker level of argument, Law and Berkeley were inclined to accept Mandeville's Augustinian account of man as a 'low' creature but criticized him for portraying men in this way because of the reprehensible practical effects such a portrait might have on men's behaviour. By denying reasonableness and by putting aside the traditional emphasis on divine sanction and punishment, these Christian moralists accused Mandeville of undermining the position of established religion. Both men were, of course, members of the clerical establishment, enraged at the impiety of the facetious[82] doctor. A recognition of what Mandeville was doing - namely attempting a descriptive ethics, should have lead them to try to disprove the basis on which he was building it - his theory of the passions. But the 'rationalists' only half-heartedly undertook this task. Their criticism thus falls well short of that of Hutcheson and Butler.

Mandeville's descriptive theory of moral behaviour involved interpreting that behaviour in terms of his egoistic psychology. Moral actions arise because of the need men have to seek the approbation of their fellows and thereby satisfy their passion of self-liking. There is therefore no contradiction between the dictates of morality and the dictates of self-interest since, given man's passionate nature, the two can coincide in producing the same action. There is also no question as to whether moral action is advantageous or not since the gratification of the uniquely important passion of self-liking had to be beneficial to the agent, whether the action seemed in his immediate interest or not.[83]

A further paradox in Mandeville's descriptive ethics is that he manages to present an account of moral behaviour, understood as other-regarding acts of agents, whilst denying the freedom of choice traditionally asserted as a necessary condition for moral actions. This is so because of the particular nature of the passion of self-liking which, as it were, automatically involves men in other-regarding action. Even when Mandeville is concerned with a purposive as opposed to instinctive behaviour, he suggests that the agent's actions are responses to passions over which he has little control. What mainly distinguishes purposive action from habitual action in the Mandevillean account is that consciousness (of the approbation of other men, whether actually forthcoming or only imagined) that accompanies it.

Mandeville's descriptive ethics is based upon his hedonistic psychology. He explains moral behaviour in terms of the approbative instinct in man. Man is a creature of his passions. Mandeville is one of those writers in the tradition of the cynics and sceptics who maintain a 'low view' of human nature. They contrast with writers who take a dignified one, stressing man's rationality and superiority to all other animals. In having this view of man as basically irrational, Mandeville was close to those <u>moraliste</u> French writers from Montaigne to Bayle whose influence we have considered. He was also following, in a secularized form, the Calvinistic notion of man's innate corruption, a feature of his thought well investigated by G S Vichert and one which I shall return to in the next chapter.[84]

One particular feature of Baylian psychology which was taken up and developed by Mandeville was that of the 'contradiction in the frame of men' which can be described as 'cognitive derangement'.[85] In the 'Remarks' he says:

'This Contradiction in the Frame of Man is the Reason that the Theory of Virtue is so well understood, and the Practice of it so rarely to be met with.'[86]

Now the 'theory of virtue' which Mandeville talks about in this passage is that ascetic and rational morality which Kaye called 'rigoristic'.[87] It consists in denying the promptings of the passions, a thing unlikely given the nature of man. Yet rigorism remains, throughout Mandeville's works, the only _substantive_ ethical code which he will allow as satisfying the criteria of judging actions to be of 'real' virtue. Because of its alleged rarity, Mandeville finds he hardly has to consider it at all. It therefore provides an escape from questions of substantive ethics.

Mandeville's psychological theory leads him to extreme scepticism as to the possibility of virtuous action in an ascetically conceived sense. Having begun with the _moraliste_ preoccupation of 'epater le bourgeois' by showing the hypocrisy of those lamenting the absence of a Christian, ascetic society or a virtuous, classical republic; his 'anatomizing' of human nature, the more serious concern of his major works, supports the conclusion that moral virtue, as he had defined it, was rarely to be found in the world.

His main interest after the early satire is to explain the phenomena of moral instincts and behaviour in terms of his theory of human nature. His theorizing is of a clinical or scientific sort and is not intended to provide the basis for any prescriptive ethical theory. It is undertaken by the detached analyst in the same spirit, as Cleomenes ironically tells us, one might undertake the examination and dissection of so lowly a creature as a mole.[88]

Mandeville's moral commentary therefore involves two distinct cosiderations - his satirical interest in exposing the inconsistency of holding two contradictory moral positions and his naturalistic interest in giving a psychological account of moral behaviour. To highlight his task in the first case, he insists upon a rigorist definition of virtue, characterising it as typically involving rational self-denial. For the second of his purposes - that is for his naturalistic theory, he maintains that virtue so rigoristically defined can never exist in the world as it is and so he seeks to explain a more mundane pursuit of 'good' in terms of his theory of approbation.

Mandeville is thus concerned with moral phenomena as a moraliste, exposing the inconsistency between men's professions and practices or as a naturalist describing the psychological conditions of moral behaviour. This being the case, he does not provide support for any sort of new moral order, though, as I have already diagnosed, he is pragmatically committed to the 'modern' developments of Augustan society. Because of this practical advocacy of the new values of economic expansionism and the suggestion that the utilitarian side of the paradox more truly accords with Mandeville's moral prescriptions, various modern critics have wished to cast him in the role of the 'philosopher of avarice'[89] or the spokesman for a new moral order justified in utilitarian terms.[90] I hope to have shown that this distracts attention from the real concerns of the moraliste and the naturalist.

Mandeville's only prescriptive exhortations are for men to be consistent in their attitudes, though his tone and mood also suggest a pragmatic acceptance of 'modern' values most easily justified in an utilitarian ethics, the conditions of which he is certainly aware.[91] But his real interest lies in an anatomy of moral behaviour. His approach to religion, our next subject, arises from the same intellectual concern.

CHAPTER V: RELIGION

At the beginning of his full-length work on religion, entitled, <u>Free Thoughts on Religion, the Church and National Happiness</u>, Mandeville defines religion as "an Acknowledgement of an Immortal Power".[1] He later says that "Men of Sense, and Good Logicians"[2] have vainly wasted their time arguing about and discussing the subject since time immemorial, for knowledge of God is something "which no Language can give them the least Idea of."[3] God is ineffable, religion must be mysterious, therefore "no Man ... ought to be too dogmatical in Matters of Faith."[4]

Mandeville thus ruled out the possibility of a rational or systematic religion on epistemological grounds: being a matter beyond human comprehension, nothing can be known about God and nothing worthwhile can be said on this subject. He leaves himself free to concentrate on what really interests him in the rest of the book, namely a general critique of religious phenomena as an aspect of human behaviour, an expose of the corrupt practices of the clergy through the ages and a plea for toleration if not permissiveness.

Mandeville's political interest in controlling the clergy (a preoccupation much flavoured by his anti-clericalism) and his examination of the origin and psychology of the religious impulse are other important themes that we have to consider. There is also the question of contemporary attacks on him, mainly targeted at his alleged 'free-thinking'.

Mandeville did not indulge in what has been described as the 'grand subterfuge'[5] of the seventeenth century - namely the avoidance of examining 'religious emotion nakedly as an aspect of human nature.'[6] His scepticism, prevented him from blanching at the blasphemous implications of taking a naturalistic approach in analysing religious behaviour. The toleration of his own society saved him from persecution.

Mandeville, as Kaye has said, lacked religious feeling.[7] He understood and indeed was steeped in the Calvinist tradition, in which grace and nature were ever divided and pleasure was set aside in favour of duty. But he did not take this Calvinistic view of things seriously. If he maintained it at all, it was for purposes of satire. When he had had his fun, he took to an analysis of religion in psychological terms, as we see from his <u>Free Thoughts</u>.

As the title of the book makes clear, Mandeville is concerned with the role of the church in national affairs, but he also raises questions about schism and the need for a spirit of toleration. The political intention of the book - namely the demand for a strict, secular control of the clergy in order to promote toleration and with it, national peace and prosperity - covers up his central preoccupation, 'anatomizing'[8] human nature. An understanding of the theological background of Calvinism together with a recognition of Mandeville's strong <u>moraliste</u> anti-clericalism, helps makes the 'political' intention of the book more intelligible and is a useful prelude to considering his examination of man's religious instincts.

One of the most striking features of the work is Mandeville's avoidance of traditional, religious controversies altogether. His grounds for evasion are that theological problems are too complicated for him or any man to solve. Men have wasted their time trying to grapple with such problems as the simultaneous oneness and trinity of God and the complex web of free-will and predestination;[9] mysteries beyond even the explanatory competence of St Paul.[10] Their insistence upon maintaining dogmatic positions has led to violent conflict. In Mandeville's native Holland, the struggle between Calvinists and Armenians illustrated the consequences of religions bigotry. In his adopted country, England, a civil war had been fought as much on religious, as on constitutional, grounds. Both historical events had exhausted civic energies. Eighteenth century toleration, which Mandeville espoused, was as much a response to the desire for peace as it was a matter of principle.

Mandeville's 'political' demand for Erastianism is couched in the anti-clerical tones of the moraliste,[11] for he says that compromise and the national peace which it brings would never be championed by the clergy:

'it is not their Interest (that) we should meet each other halfway more than it would be the Interest of a Ferryman to have the two Shores unite.'[12]

Even when one clerical faction has broken from another, as happened in the Reformation, that faction itself soon divides into warring parts despite the efforts of Princes and others to prevent it.[13] Mandeville's explanations for these occurrences is couched in characteristically psychological language:

'The generality of Men are so wedded to and so obstinately fond of their own Opinion and Doctrine they have been imbued with from their Cradle, that they cannot think anyone sincere, who being acquainted with it, refuses to embrace it.'[14]

Given this fact about human nature and the corrupting influence of power and success, the clergy cannot be expected to advocate toleration themselves.[15] Indeed since only total suppression eliminates schism, they can only be expected to engage in violent and divisive activities. Toleration must therefore be imposed from without by the civil authorities. Mandeville therefore stresses, particularly in the last two chapters of Free

Thoughts, the necessity for obedience to the sovereign secular power.

Mandeville's anti-clericalism also manifests itself in a continuous expose of the vicious practices of clergy through the ages, particularly those of members of the Roman Catholic Church.[16] These clerical practices have been based on a thorough understanding of human psychology and involve an exploitation of human frailty.[17] The original spirit of Christianity, simple and unaffected, was deliberately set aside and replaced by the pomp of Popery. Instead of being practised at home or in open places, Christianity was practiced in magnificent churches, for the clergy realized that

'There is a kind of Magick in a fine Church. They (ie. men) look upon it as a Rampart against Hell and the Devil.'[18]

Mandeville does not hazard a guess as to the historical period when large-scale sophistication of Christian practices began,[19] but he does consider the considerable influence of 'the gaudy shew and pompous ceremonies of triumphant paganism.'[20] Paganism encouraged an interest in the 'Outward show',[21] and the Christian emphasis on the ceremonial and symbolic, was often an extension of that mentality. There was no scriptural authority for many of the Church's rites. Eventually the pomp of the Mass, the richness of priests' garments and equipages, the emphasis on fine statues and works of art and the superstitious reverence for symbols such as the cross became the mainstay of Catholic and therefore, Christian, worship. The Reformation, brought about by people protesting against these fineries and superstitions, was itself corrupted. The Church of England gave dogmatic emphasis to matters of ceremony and Church etiquette.[22]

If Mandeville wanted a firm secular control of all clergies, it was not because he underrated the immense influence that religion could have on the unity of a nation. He is at pains to make the point, many times,[23] that:

'without the Belief of an invisible Cause, no Man's Word is to be relied upon, no Vows or Protestations can be depended upon; but as soon as a Man believes, that there is a Power somewhere, that will certainly punish him, if he forswears himself; as soon, I say, as a Man believes this, we have Reason to trust to his Oath; at least, it is a better Test than any other Verbal Assurance.'[24]

Religious belief thereby underpins important contractual commitments without which life in civil society simply could not exist. What particular character the religious impulse expressed was of no great importance, so long as it was not divisive. The important point about religious adherence was that if made men feel they were bound to keep promises and contracts.[25] Even a sceptic could understand that.

Mandeville turns from the political aspect of religion and the the control of the clergy (who set themselves up to interpret matters beyond human comprehension[26]) to analysing religious behaviour in psychological terms. He considers the reasons that induce men to accept ideas contrary to reason and their senses, commenting:

'... were Men to be taught from the Infancy that it was a Mystery, that on a certain occasion Two and Two made Seven, with an addition to be believ'd on pain of Damnation, I am persuaded that at least Seven in Ten would swallow the shameful Paradox ...'[27]

Mysteries are therefore accepted because men have been taught to accept them from childhood. The fact that they contradict reason is insufficient grounds for rejection: habitual behaviour needs no specific justification.

Mandeville's analysis of free-will provides another illustration of his treatment of religion from the psychological, rather than from the theological, point of view. In this case he asserts the propostion that theological arguments are too complex and are, in any case, irresoluble. There is therefore nothing to be gained from a prolonged examination of what must be highly speculative opinions. One is better employed actually looking into what is meant by behaving freely. And that investigation establishes that the wish to be free is not the same as the ability to be so.[28] Whatever they wish, men are guided by their passions out of a 'fatal and unvoidable necessity'.[29]

From questions of dogma treated psychologically, we find Mandeville's attention directed to the concrete symbols and rites of the Church[30] which the clergy use to assuage mankind's need for re-assurance. In the Christian church, the most important symbol is the cross. Mandeville considers that when used excessively, as in the Catholic Church, or totally excluded as in the Protestant, the symbol of the cross has mistakenly been made an object (possibly superstitious) of attention rather than a mere convenience for representing the ideas or moods of the faith. Nevertheless the use of symbols of this sort does evoke certain responses and attitudes, a matter well understood by the clergy of all faiths. The use of garments specially consecrated, or incense and the varied statutery of Catholicism play a similarly important part in ritual. Objects of this sort are designed to inspire awe and a sense of solemnity and holiness which particularly impresses the feeble-minded. Yet Mandeville says, rather cynically, that priest's robes are no:

'More holy or more necessary than the Gowns of Judges, the Swordbearer's Cap of Maintenance or the Habits of the Yeomen of the Guards ...'[31]

Mandeville adopts the same <u>libertin</u> attitude to ceremonies of the church like the mass which enshrines the greatest mysteries of the Christian faith. These mysteries 'transcend reason',[32] they are accepted instinctively rather than on any intellectual grounds. The only authority for them is scriptural and they cannot, therefore, be measured by the standards of reason. Mandeville would have agreed with Voltaire's dictum that 'reason must not utter a single word when faith speaks.'[33] and he did a good deal to launch the sceptical attack on Christianity itself, hitherto accorded a special place above other religions. He is unsparing when applying the logic of scepticism to Christianity, as his words show us:

'Experience teaches us that this opinion (ie. the acceptance of mysteries) is much influenced by the Fears, wishes, inclinations and varies according to the capacity of the believer.'[34]

Mandeville maintains that all religious instinct, including the Christian one, is based on the fear man has of death and the fear he has of the unknown.[35] The first of these fears is more easily assuaged. Certain safeguards in the 'mechanism of man'[36] protect him from dwelling obsessively on his fate by concentrating his mind on the struggle to survive.[37] The second fear, that of the unknown, is more difficult to temper since the constant incomprehensibility of his environment provides man with a constant reminder of it. In the savage 'state of nature' this fear is pervasive for any 'mischief' or 'disaster' that happens to man:

'of which the Cause is not very plain and obvious; excessive Heat and Cold; Wet and Drought, that are offensive; Thunder and Lightning; Noises in the dark, Obscurity itself, and everything that is frightful and unknown, are all administering and contributing to the Establishment of this Fear.'[38]

As man became more used to ordering his thoughts, his jumbled ideas of an 'invisible power' would begin to take a more settled form. The outline or code of a religion would emerge. Eventually a body of men, the priests, would establish themselves as interpreters of the divine order.

Although he does not develop a thorough-going 'imposture theory' of the sort Fontenelle had applied to paganism,[39] Mandeville does tend to see the development of religion as the development of a 'source of power for ... politicians and their priestly corps'.[40] A good deal of Free Thoughts is taken up with decrying the 'Tricks and Stratagems of Cleric Invention'[41] applicable to Christianity as much as to paganism, a development of the Baylian position. In Part II of the Fable,[42] Mandeville makes Cleomenes distinguish carefully between the idolatry of pagan religions and the logical application of the analysis to Christianity as well as paganism, leaving the reader in no doubt that in making such an application he follows Mandeville's own intentions. Christianity, as much as any other religion, is based upon fear. Its exploitation by those in charge of religion is a legitimate and important exercise when it is directed, as Mandeville recognized it could be in a significant way, toward the national welfare.

Bayle's influence upon Mandeville's religious writing is still manifest in his last important work, namely the Origin of Honour, 1732, published over a decade after Free Thoughts. If Mandeville's concern in Free Thoughts is with a pathology of the religious instinct in man, as well as in the political object of controlling the clergy, in the Origin of Honour it is with the question of how men manage to reconcile their religious beliefs with their behaviour - both pychological themes which would have interested his precursor, the 'philosopher of Rotterdam'.[43] Bayle had held back from applying his critique of paganism to Christianity, leaving Christian theology in a privileged position. Mandeville, understanding the implicit lesson that Bayle's argument that Christianity would also be subject to sceptical strictures, did not hesitate to extend the argument. Mandeville gave Bayle's notorious paradox that atheism was more acceptable to God than pagan idolatory a further twist by saying that many atheists lead better lives than many Christians.[44] These 'atheists' (a term Mandeville believed should only be used to describe self-confessed disbelievers) were 'speculative atheists',[45] they were 'quiet, moral men'[46] who acted out of genuine conviction rather than as an excuse for licentiousness. They should be respected for their intellectual courage. Little wonder Mandeville became the bogeyman of the clerics expressing opinions of this sort.

In the Origin of Honour Mandeville again takes up the theme of human contradiction, of man, as he had said in The Fable, acting 'most commonly against his Principles'.[47] In this later work Mandeville satirizes the inconsistency which enables men to claim to be Christians, devoted to an other-worldly and benevolent philosophy whilst at the same time insisting on their role as 'men of honour', regulated by a martial code. Christianity and honour are opposed: Christianity encourages conciliation and forgiveness, honour demands confrontation and the satisfaction of revenge. Christianity, properly understood, cannot be useful for war, though the exhortations of priests and their manipulation of symbols and language have and do contribute to the success of particular military ventures.[48]

Duelling is one feature of the code of honour which illustrates how impossible it is to be a man of honour and a true Christian at the same time.[49] By conventional codes, a man whose honour has been challenged, must seek to defend it by duelling. An elaborate system of rules has arisen to regulate the practice in European society. But however closely a man of honour follows these rules, he is behaving in an unChristian way, for Christianity condemns the shedding of blood. Because men try to reconcile these diverse attitudes,

'The practice of nominal Christians is perpetually clashing with the theory they profess.'[50]

The demands of the 'theory they profess' are in fact, unrealistic because they require qualities in human nature which are not there. Truly Christian behaviour would involve restraining man's passion, or 'vital motion',[51] that energy which brings life to the 'lumpish machine.'[52] Honour, on the other hand, involves stirring up men's passions, particularly their self-liking. It thus makes no unnatural demand of man. Politicians and their clerical allies realize this: they encourage unchristian notions of honour and martial glory in the name of national interest or the public good. Mandeville has no hesitation in showing the distinctly Machiavellian uses that may be made of the religious impulse in backing national greatness. He insists, mischievously, that when a Christian Prince takes such an action, he contradicts the tenets of his own faith,

Mandeville's pretence at holding to a strict definition of 'Christian' behaviour has led at least one modern scholar, E J Chiasson,[53] to identify him in the 'massive but flexible'[54] tradition of Christian humanism in which the need for grace and regeneration are paramount. Chiasson says:

'the suppostion that Mandeville could seriously propose embracing _either_ the world _or_ religion is a serious misunderstanding of what he means by both terms. For just as he recognizes in his philosophy of man that grace is given to nature to regenerate it, so he recognizes, in his social philosophy, that the purely secular state is a truncated version of what the state might be if grace and revelation were permitted to perform their illuminating function.'[55]

Chiasson's claim is no less than an assertion that Mandeville had a genuine theological interest, a viewpoint hardly borne out by the extended discussions of religious pathology we find in all the texts.

Where Chiasson does quote from Mandeville to support his argument, he seems to ignore the context from which his selected passaged are to be found. He instances Mandeville's reference to an 'infinite and eternal being' as evidence of his belief in the supernatural, failing to point out that this reference is in the context of Mandeville's exploration of the development of a religious instinct in 'savage man'. Mandeville's concern in that part of the Fable was with a conjectural history of religion; he was exploring its evolution as an established social institution. He is typically exploring the psychological origin of religion; he is not asserting any theological doctrine.[56]

Chiasson further maintains that reference to man's obligation to God is proof of Mandeville's religious faith. But the words occur in a passage where Mandeville considers, in an anthropological way, how men progressed from 'paying his respects to the Tree he gathers his Nuts from'[57] to belonging to an established religion. To suggest this is an expression of Mandeville's own faith is an absurd distortion.

Chiasson seems intent on saving Mandeville from that Calvinist tradition which stressed the separation of grace and nature and taught that a minority, the elect, were predestined to receive grace. Instead he wants to place him in a wider stream of Christian humanism whose advocates had always concerned themselves with man as a social being. This object is unconvincing and in the end Chiasson seems to provide his own refutation by saying that Mandeville's 'patience with the immoralities of men seems to result from his tendency to look at these matters from the point of view of a sociologist rather than a moralist'.[58]

Chiasson's conclusion reminds us that it is misleading to represent Mandeville as the exponent of a doctrinal point of view. G S Vichert has made the point that:

'Bayle's view of man is darker and sterner than Mandeville's but the difference is only of degree. Immediately behind both of them stands the words of the Heidelberg catechism.'[59]

But in Mandeville's case the Calvinist element is highly secularized. He has no intrinsic interest in doctrinal matters and shows a total disinterest in the subject of the good life as a preparation for salvation. He has inherited the harshness of Calvin's view of man's situation without even the hope of a better future life. As one modern scholar has pointed out when Mandeville is closest to Calvinism, he is often at his most cynical.[60]

Mandeville's evident anti-clericalism, his 'scientific' treatment of religious subjects and his obvious lack of religious seriousness increasingly made him the object of clerical attacks in the eighteenth century. This was particularly the case after the 'second[61] edition of the *Fable*, to which is appended the notorious 'Essay on Charity and Charity Schools,' in which Mandeville attacked the usefulness of these institutions as well as the motives of those who supported them. Mandeville's notoriety was assured by the condemnation of the *Fable* by the Grand Jury of Middlesex to whom the book had been 'presented' as a menace to public morals. The Grand Jury alleged that the book was a propagation of infidelity, a corruption of moral and religious standards and an undermining of governmental authority which was based upon religion.[62] This latter point was seized upon by various early critics, such as the anonymous author of the 'Letter To Lord C' which appeared in the *London Journal*.[63] Mandeville was called a 'British Catiline'[64] and a dire warning was given against:

'This profligate Author of the Fable (who) is not only an Auxiliary to Catiline in Opposition to Faith but has taken upon him to tear up the very Foundations of Moral Virtue, and establish Vice in its Room.'[65]

The bitterness of this anonymous attack is taken up by other contemporaries. Dennis begins libelling the impious author of the *Fable*, by saying that whilst in the past there had been many champions for deism, socinianism, and arianism; they had all made their attacks in the name of moral virtue; whereas:

'a champion for vice and luxury, a serious, a cool, a deliberate champion, that is a creature entirely new, and has never been heard of before in any nation, or in any age of the world.'[66]

Like the author of the 'Letter to Lord C', Dennis was most outraged by Mandeville's attack on Charity Schools.[67] This seemed to him, as well as to other clerical proponents of the charity system, to be an impious attack on institutions dedicated to propagating Christianity among the poor. The effects of closing the schools would be drastic. Dennis missed the chance to tackle Mandeville's arguments on private vices, public benefits more fully by being diverted into the mere labelling of its author as a libertin. His evident distaste for Mandeville's style and tone made it difficult for him to attack his opponent in a clear headed way.

William Law, another cleric, should have been a more formidable adversary but he too found it difficult to get away from his strident criticism of that 'depravity'[68] which he claimed was inherent in Mandeville's paradox. Law realized that to refute Mandeville, one would have to disprove his psychological assumptions, his 'painting of men like brutes',[69] but all he did was merely to assert the self-evident rationality of man, a fact as 'plain as that we have bodies and senses.'[70] That men act according to passion and not reason <u>at certain times</u> is no proof against this rationality in Law's eyes. God had so designed man that by the use of his reason he was able to discover the eternal and immutable truths about nature. These 'truths' were as much about the moral, as the physical, structure of reality. Having taken this stance, Law examines certain parts of the <u>Fable</u> with painstaking literalness: the state of nature could not have existed since it is a state which the 'scriptures makes morally impossible that Men should ever have been in'.[71]

Of Mandeville's allegorical account of the origin of morality and the role of the 'lawgivers and other wise men',[72] Law says, with rather heavy irony,

'One would think that you had been an eye witness to all that passed, and that you had held the candle to those first philosophers when they were so carefully peeping into human nature. You do not love to dwell upon little matters, or else you could have told us the philospher's name who first discovered this flattery, how long he looked before he found it, how he proved it to be agreeable to pride, what disputes happenedd upon the occasion, and how many ages of the world had passed before this consultation of the philosophers.'[73]

Law's comments on the Fable were made in 1724, before the appearance of the second part of the book in 1729 and he could not therefore have taken account of the evolutionary treatment of religion given in that latter part. However, his insistence on reading Mandeville as one of the 'sagacious advocates for immorality',[74] rendered his analysis of the first part of the Fable superficial and defective.

One of Mandeville's most distinguished clerical crtics was Bishop Berkeley. His Alciphron was a refutation of all those 'minute philosophers'[75] who, in the bishop's opinion, were undermining religion by their advocacy of libertinism. It has been said of Berkeley that he

'firmly believed (as people often do) that his own age surpassed most others in vice and depravity, in the reckless pursuit of pleasure, in the wanton neglect of private and public duty.'[76]

He was therefore 'sincerely and perhaps predominantly concerned to defeat what he took to be the irreligious, even atheistic tendencies of his age.'[77]

Berkeley's view was that these tendencies had resulted from the mechanical philosophies of Hobbes, Newton[78] and Locke, all of which were thoroughly materialistic. His philosophical idealism was a challenge, as he saw it, to that mechanico-materialism and he ingenously supported it by developing Locke's own theory of perception. Berkeley regarded Mandeville as a 'market place' purveyor of these heretical theories, and in stressing the irrational qualities of man as an apologist for uncontrolled and licentious behaviour.[79] According to Berkeley, the rational capacity of humans was what distinguished them from all other creatures. Since the differentiating quality of any object or being was its essential nature (the thing that defined it), rationality was essential to man's nature. Man was naturally a rational being. The non-rational senses or passions were the 'lowest part or faculty of the human soul'.[80] In their myopia, the 'Minute Philosphers' emphasized this 'lowest part' and condemned man to the bestial condition of any animal of uncontrollable passions.

Furthermore, Berkeley ridicules the 'Minute Philosophers' for believing that, at a stroke they have 'demolished the whole fabric of humane folly and superstition.'[81] They believe that by calling attention to the existence of the various religions in the world, they have shown how futile it is to hold a religious belief. They falsely imagine they have proved an inconsistancy in man's intellect. Rather than that, the Bishop maintains, the existence of religion at all stages of human history shows an uniformity. Men of religion have sought to understand good and absolute truth. Whatever their conclusions, these 'immutables' have remained.[82] The 'Minute Philosophers' are condemned as relativists, who covertly aim at supporting libertinism so as to justify their own debauched existences.[83]

Berkeley was particularly offended by the challenge he saw in Mandeville's paradoxical assertion of 'private vices, public benefits'.[84] Like other 'Minute Philosophers', Mandeville seemed to him to be designing to make people 'wicked upon principle'[85] and attempting a libertine justification of immoral living. He missed Mandeville's satirical intention of exposing contradictory attitudes amongst contemporaries who professed Christianity but practiced 'good living'. Berkeley read the <u>Fable</u> as a literal prescription for the indulgence of vice and luxury. Like the critics we have already considered, Berkeley fell into the trap of Mandeville's satirical snares and never extricated himself or tackled his substantive assertions about human nature more convincingly. Most clerical critics concentrated on the threats they saw in Mandeville's work to established religion rather than on his assessment of human nature or his psychology of religion.[86] To some extent this task would have been made more difficult because they shared Mandeville's view of man as a 'fallen creature'. Their outcry was shriller because they believed Mandeville was publicizing certain 'truths' about human nature which had to be corrected rather than dwelt upon.[87]

Mandeville himself was not unaware of the provocation he afforded the clergy which, we are told, entered his conversation as well as his writing.[88] For despite his serious concern with examining religious phenomena in the light of human psychology in <u>Free Thoughts</u> and the <u>Origin of Honour</u>, Mandeville was also a satirist concerned with poking fun at and exposing the folly of, his fellow creatures. Lovejoy alludes[89] to the practice of 'epater le bourgeois'; a well established 'sport' among those French <u>moraliste</u> predecessors of Mandeville's. The clergy were one of the professions constantly ridiculed (the medical corps, among whom Mandeville himself ranked, was another), and a robust anti-clericalism is a hallmark of this satirical genre. The 'Grumbling Hive' is written very much in the _libertin_ spirit; one of its purposes being to expose the way that professional men live off the vices of their fellows.

An amusing expression of this anti-clericalism is to be found in Mandeville's parable of 'small beer'.[90] The clergy allow that 'small beer' may be drunk so long as men do it only to 'mend their complexions.' If they drink it for pleausre, they indulge in vice which cannot in anyway be condoned. But the clergy are sufficiently skilled in casuistry to persuade the authorities that given this distinction, there can be no harm in allowing men a particularly harmless indulgence.

Jacob Viner has argued that it is essential, in judging the seriousness of Mandeville's work, to recognize the _moraliste_ tone in his early writing so that we are not lead into a fruitless debate about whether he was ingenuous or not on various doctrinal matters. Indeed Viner says that there can be no doubt about Mandeville's insincerity, his advocacy of unqualified rigorism has to be recognized as an essential ingredient of his satire.[91]

Mandeville remains ambivalent on most substantial religious questions long after he has ceased to be primarily concerned with satire.[92] While he at first insists on ridiculing inconsistency; he later concentrates on setting religious belief in the context of an extended review of human psychology. It may be tantalizing for us to be left in doubt about Mandeville's own belief or lack of it but it is a doubt that in no way interferes with our more proper appreciation of the value of his psychological analysis. Not only is it easier to accept his view that no one should be condemned an atheist unless he admits to it, it is also unnecessary to dwell on questions that do not affect our judgement of his contribution to Hume's 'science of man'. The thrust of this book has been to redirect attention to that contribution, one which any reader of Mandeville's works must recognize as considerable.

CHAPTER VI: CONCLUSION

Bernard Mandeville's writing spans a period of almost fifty years. Among his literary output can be found works of many genres: theses, translations, tracts, verse, essays and books. His use of literary devices ranges from fables, dialogues and satire, to irony and paradox. He is concerned with many subjects - politics, economics, social theory, morality, religion, medicine and psychology. This diverse range of presentation and subject matter makes Mandeville a particularly difficult writer to classify. More seriously, it casts doubts upon his coherency and intentions as a thinker. His status as a serious writer has been undermined by the continuous debate as to whether he was a libertine or not. The 'succès de scandale' which the <u>Fable</u> achieved has never quite disappeared from his critics' thoughts.[1]

What can we learn from Mandeville himself of his own intentions? He declares two ambitions. The first is to expose hypocrites and those holding to inconsistent moral positions. The second is to 'anatomize'[2] (ie. analyse) human nature.

Mandeville's satirical intention has its most pungent expression in the 'Grumbling Hive' but it is evident in both parts of the <u>Fable</u>;[3] in <u>Free Thoughts</u>;[4] in the <u>Origin of Honour</u>[5] and also in <u>Dion</u>.[6] In the 'Grumbling Hive', he seeks to expose those bees (the hypocrites) who enjoy the (material) benefits of worldly greatness whilst at the same time deploring the absence of simple, virtuous living. He enjoys the paradox that results from linking material wealth to the indulgence of human passions, like pride and avarice, traditionally understood by moralists as 'vices'. By highlighting the difficulties that arise if men attempt to maintain different ethical standards at the same time, Mandeville makes an early contribution to the important eighteenth century debate about the relationship between material progress and moral decline.

His other self-declared interest in in 'anatomizing the invisible Part of Man', or seeking to explain the elaborate workings of human nature. His psychological egoism and mechanical theory of the passions are the major contributions he makes to the development of human psychology.

Mandeville is thus self-consciously satirical and scientific. Nor are his two concerns unrelated. His early intention as a satirist, to expose false pretensions, was made with an implicit view of human nature in mind. According to that view, man was a creature of the passions, who, could seldom rise to the demands of virtue, understood as rigorous self-denial. Mandeville the satirist thus set out to show the folly of men who ignored what Mandeville the 'anatomist' or scientist was later to investigate in considerable detail and with considerable subtlety.

The object of Mandeville's satire and the object of his psychological investigations amount to the same pursuit after the truth about human nature as he saw it. Those who ignored the facts about man as a creature of his passions needed to be instructed. Everyone would then realize and admit that the passions, 'commonly call'd frailties' are, in fact, the 'very Powers that govern the whole Machine.'[7]

Sometimes he enlists the help of spokesmen like the 'Oxford Gentleman' in the <u>Female Tatlers</u> or Cleomenes and Horatio in Part II of the Fable and the <u>Origin of Honour</u>. His psychological preoccupation is evident even in works given over to other specific subjects, like the <u>Hypocondriack and Hysterick Passions</u>, the medical treatise on his professional speciality and in minor works like the <u>Stews</u> or <u>Tyburn</u> where he examines the problems of prostitution and crime respectively. Social structures and arrangements are considered in the light of the psychological knowledge of man in the <u>Female Tatlers</u>, the <u>Fable</u>, <u>Free Thoughts</u> and the <u>Origin of Honour</u>. Whatever particular moral, religious or economic themes he is considering, Mandeville's view of man as a creature of his passions is always in the background of his thinking.

The consistency of Mandeville's interest in psychology does not mean that he did not change his views on particular matters. We have seen how he refined his early concept of pride by later distinguishing self-love from self-liking;[8] how he more carefully develops his account of social evolution in Part II of the Fable supplementing the allegory of the 'lawgivers and other wise men' of Part I; and how his treatment of morality becomes more naturalistic and less polemical. Nor should his pre-occupation with exposing human frailty, leave us unaware of certain limitations in his thought as a whole.

These limitations result from the fundamentalist and mundane nature of that thought. His fundamentalism, that is his treatment of everything from the point of view of psychology can be criticized on the grounds that it minimizes the importance of other factors, like economic and political ones. And his particular kind of psychological theory, that of individualism, may be said to underestimate the importance of groups and classes acting as social forces or the particular and historical context, rather than the general abstract background, of a social situation.[9]

His mundanity, characteristically eighteenth century, means that he fails to develop a metaphysics or wider philosophical context in which to interpret this theory of human nature and society. Such a context is only hinted at.

Mandeville's deficiency as a philospher in a fully-fledged sense is aggravated by his lack of serious epistemology and his essayist style of writing.[10] In principle he subscribes to Locke's empiricism, deploring a priori speculation unsubstantiated by empirical evidence. But he does not expound upon his method, scientific though his analytic intentions were. His ideas are developed and his interest in exploring human nature is sustained but he never becomes systematic or self-consciously restrained in his use of language. To gather what he says about any subject, we have to expore the texts of works and synthesise on his behalf.

Nevertheless despite these limitations I hope to have shown that Mandeville's thought can be read coherently and that within the areas of human psychology and social arrangements, he intended to be and was, consistent. Nor should his undoubted importance influence upon various aspects of eighteenth century thought be underrated.

Mandeville's most important contribution is in his elaboration of psychological theory. No one had pursued egoism so thoroughly as a way of explaining human motivation and social structures. Though Mandeville owed a lot to predecessors like Hobbes and the French sceptics, his presentation of these themes is original in its intricacy and relevance to the evolution of social institutions.

His analysis of the evolution of society is another important contribution he made to the study of society. In the <u>Fable</u> especially in Part II, we find one of the earliest examples of an extended anthropological kind of theorizing that became labelled 'philosophic' or conjectural history by the great Enlightenment <u>philosophes</u>, British as well as French.[11]

Kaye analysed Mandeville's impact on moral philosophy. In effect, he posed a dilemma between utilitarian and rationalistic ethics:- Hume developed the utilitarian, whilst Kant developed the rationalistic choice that the Mandevillean paradox presented. By juxtapositioning opposites in the way he did, Mandeville stimulated the long eighteenth century debate on material progress and moral decline, a subject enthusiastically taken up by Rousseau.

Different modern scholars have drawn attention to other important features of Mandeville's thought. He has traditionally been given an important place in the development of classical, laissez-faire economics, his name being linked with Adam Smith's.[12] He had been regarded as an interesting political theorist,[13] and an important forerunner of sociology.[14] Few critics have ever underrated the literary quality of his work.[15]

The influences which contributed to his eclecticism were various. They included the French sceptical tradition, represented by writers from Montaigne to Bayle. Bayle's influence was of great importance but we also find ideas from the English philosophers Hobbes and Locke. Kaye includes Erasmus, Spinoza and early writers on economic subjects such as Culpepper, Child and Barbon as intellectual ancestors of Mandeville's.

It has been said of Rochefoucauld that he assumed the 'vantage of a seignorial detachment' and played the roles of 'spectator, psychologist and stylist'.[16] Because Mandeville did the same, he has been dismissed as a mere literateur. I hope to have shown that Mandeville's thought is more substantial than that of a mere essayist and that it is sufficiently coherent to justify Hume's perceptive and considerable compliment in placing him among those

'late philosophers in England, who have begun to put the science of man on a new footing, and have engaged the attention, and excited the curiosity of the public.'[17]

APPENDIX I

Note on Mandeville as a Medical Doctor.[1]

Mandeville was by profession a medical doctor who specialised in diseases of the stomach and nervous disorders, or in his own language, in the "Hypocondriack and hysterick passions."[2] This certainly did not mean that he spared the profession from his satire; in the 'Grumbling Hive' he retorts:

"Physicians valu'd Fame and Wealth
Above the dropping Patient's Health
Or their own Skill: The greatest Part
Study'd, instead of Rules of Art,
Grave pensive Looks and dull Behaviour,
To gain'th 'Apothecary's Favour;
The Praise of Mid-wives, Priests and all
That serv'd at Birth or Funeral ..."[3]

This satirical treatment of the profession is in the French tradition, in particular the tradition of Fontaine's 'Les Medicins'[4] which Mandeville translated in his collection of fables entitled 'Aesop Dress'd'.[5] Rather more serious criticism came in his full-length medical work; "A Treatise on the Hypocondriack and Hysterick Passions".(1711)

Kaye tells us that medicine was the traditional profession of Mandeville's family[6] and that his father had even specialized in the same field as he himself was to do. One of the early indications of this interest appears in his Oratio Scholastica(1685) which was Mandeville's matriculation thesis writen while he was at the Erasmian School at Rotterdam. In the thesis he states his intention to devote himself to medicine. The need for a careful study of anatomy and the uses of drugs and medicines is essential for the promotion of sound physical and mental health.

Once at the University of Leiden, Mandeville seems to have pursued a course in philosophy as well as in medicine.[7] He produced on philosophic dissertion on the question of animal automatism although his doctoral thesis <u>Disputatio Medica Inauguralis de Chyliosi. Leiden 1691</u>, was on the subject of maldigestion and nervous disorders of the stomach. He said in defence of the subject matter:

"Thinking of what material I should examine, I defend my choice of the working of chylification (digestion) because the bad effects of it (when disordered) can be seen everywhere and many serious illnesses have their origin in this source".[8]

In this thesis he considers various theories about the causes of stomach disorders and gives his own opinion that amongst them can be counted nervous upsets. In general he stresses the psychological factor in such disorders, observing that patients have been able to eat what would otherwise be harmful to them because they have believed that they needed a particular food. He notices loss of appetite when a patient has had bad news. Stomach 'fermentation' is disrupted when, for some reason, the nerves in the stomach upset the balance of digestive juices.[9]

By Mandeville's lifetime, Leiden had succeeded Padua as the leading medical centre of Europe and the Dutch universities generally had become the foremost institutes of medicine.[10] At the time when Mandeville was in his first year at the university a distinguished foreign doctor using the name of Van Linden visited the university for a month - Van Linden was John Locke. After he graduated and began practising, Mandeville became a strong advocate for the 'empirical method' in medicine and thereby followed the English school of Sydenham and Locke.

Soon after qualifying Mandeville left Holand and settled in London. His own account of his move gives us the reason for his staying away from his native land:

"Philipirio (ie. Mandeville) is a foreigner and a physician who, after he had finished his studies and taken his degree beyond sea, was come to London to learn the language; in which having happened to take great delight, and in the meantime found the country and the manners of it agreeable to his humour, as he has now been many years, and is like to end his days in England."[11]

In London he practised his specialization - the 'hypocondriack and hysterick passions' and some years later (in 1711) before his extension of the Grumbling Hive into the Fable, he produced a full length treatise on the subject.

The treatise begins with a lengthy defence of the 'empirical' method which remains as much his theme as specific matters connected with nervous stomach disorders. He is against the prevailing practice of his day which was for doctors to speculate abstractly about diseases. He despises doctors who pretend to be able to

"cure all manner of distempers in their closets without ever seeing a patient."[12]

It is an approach that has descredited medicine leading Mandeville to joke:

"We may conclude that the art of physick is no more to be depended upon that that of astrology"[13]

The great need, Mandeville says, is to do away with florid speculation and abstract hypothefication[14] which has contributed only to making medicine 'modish' instead of effective. He argues amusingly:

"In some of our modern hypothesis there is as much wit to be discovered as in a tolerable play and the contrivance of them costs as much labour; what a pity it is they won't cure sick people."[15]

Elaborate theories were developed on the flimsiest evidence, doctors concentrating on amassing wealth and acquiring fame instead of curing the sick.[16] Physicians should be less concerned with being stylish and concentrate on the drudgery of careful observation and practice based on experience. This might take them away from the lofty levels of Newtonian sicence,[17] but it would not reduce their usefulness to society.

Mandeville settles down to considering the symptoms of 'hypocondriack and hysterick' diseases in the Treatise; diseases in which he specialized and which he considered as primarily a result of a nervous disturbance of digestion. He calls the nerves 'internuncii'; they link the stomach to the brain:

"We know that abundance of nerve ends empty themselves into the stomach, whose inner coat is wholly nervous and yet not allowed to have any spontaneous motion of its own."[18]

Difficulties arise when, for various reasons, the nervous system of the patient is disordered and his digestion is consequently disrupted. In this condition patients display the symptoms of the 'hypocondriack and hysterick' diseases. In this way Mandeville develops the original thesis he proposed in the de Chylosi Vitiata, now confirming it by experience and stressing the close connection between the mental and emotional state of the patient and his physical health. His examples are numerous and include the effects of receiving of bad news on the appetite and of the close relation of dreams to our physical state. Of dreams, he says:

"Experience teaches us, that our having either delightful, or else troublesome dreams, is not a thing fortuitous, as the generality of people imagine, and it is demonstrable that it depends immediately upon the tone and contexture of the spirits and consequently in a great measure upon the disposition of our bodies."[19]

Taking up the current argument between the physicians and the apothecaries[20] in the profession, Mandeville's empirical bias gives him some sympathy with the latter, who often had much more practical experience than the physicians especially those who have spent their time at one of the Universities of which Mandeville did not think highly.

K Dewhurst says of this dispute:

"The dispute was really a mercenary one. Traditionally apothecaries were suppose to limit themselves to making up medicines from physicians' prescriptions, but during the seventeenth century they began to practice on their own, as they quickly acquired sufficient diagnostic skill by treating the sick poor. The physicians livelihood was threatened in 1687 when their college recommended members to give free advice to the sick and poor of London."[21]

We have already remarked on Mandeville's criticism of the medical profession for its money-grubbing which he linked to the pretence of practising a 'modish' art. His suspicion on this score no doubt re-inforced his sympathy for the apothecaries.

Does Mandeville's medical background affect his literary work?

In considering Locke's reasons for taking up medicine, Letwin[22] says that the profession was attractive for a number of reasons. Firstly medicine was detached from the controversial areas of politics and theology. Secondly, in medicine, fanaticism and faction had no place and advocates of the 'new philosophy' were not so given "to abstaining from political controversy as they were to abhorring the intrusion of enthusiasm into it"; thirdly, the financial gain of doctors was considerable.

No doubt some of these reasons can be considered to apply to Mandeville - certainly he was a bitter enemy of religious fanaticism and expressed a certain dislike for party faction. He was also against what he regarded as the undue influence of classical learning, thus allying himself with the Moderns in the battle between them and the Ancients. His family background showed him the material rewards of a successful medical career.

Various ideas and attitudes Mandeville took toward medicine are reflected in his wider works. One of the most important was his insistence on empiricism - his constant belief that it is only from experience that we gain most practical and useful knowledge. This attitude affected his psychological and his social theory. Much of his 'theorizing' is based on a kind of 'case studying' and he applies many medical analogies to the state of society, including states of advanced 'disease' or breakdown.

It is difficult to determine how large Mandeville's own practice was. A busy literary career must have limited it although Kaye maintains that his correspondence with Sir Hans Sloane, leading physician of the day, indicates an important, fashionable practice. No doubt as his book sold, he became less dependent on his medical income. In the __Treatise__, he explains his philosophical approach to medical practice:

"I hate a crowd, and I hate to be in a hurry. Besides I am naturally slow and could no more attend a dozen patients in a day and think of them as I should, than I could fly. I must own to you likewise, that I am a little selfish and can't help minding my own

"In some of our modern hypothesis there is as much wit to be discovered as in a tolerable play and the contrivance of them costs as much labour; what a pity it is they won't cure sick people."[15]

Elaborate theories were developed on the flimsiest evidence, doctors concentrating on amassing wealth and acquiring fame instead of curing the sick.[16] Physicians should be less concerned with being stylish and concentrate on the drudgery of careful observation and practice based on experience. This might take them away from the lofty levels of Newtonian sicence,[17] but it would not reduce their usefulness to society.

Mandeville settles down to considering the symptoms of 'hypocondriack and hysterick' diseases in the Treatise; diseases in which he specialized and which he considered as primarily a result of a nervous disturbance of digestion. He calls the nerves 'internuncii'; they link the stomach to the brain:

"We know that abundance of nerve ends empty themselves into the stomach, whose inner coat is wholly nervous and yet not allowed to have any spontaneous motion of its own."[18]

Difficulties arise when, for various reasons, the nervous system of the patient is disordered and his digestion is consequently disrupted. In this condition patients display the symptoms of the 'hypocondriack and hysterick' diseases. In this way Mandeville develops the original thesis he proposed in the de Chylosi Vitiata, now confirming it by experience and stressing the close connection between the mental and emotional state of the patient and his physical health. His examples are numerous and include the effects of receiving of bad news on the appetite and of the close relation of dreams to our physical state. Of dreams, he says:

APPENDIX II

'Animal Automatism' and Mandeville's Views

The question of animal automatism, or whether animals can feel or think of have 'souls' like human beings, was well known to classical philosophers and continued to be of interest up to Mandeville's own lifetime. The subject is especially interesting when considered in the context of Mandeville's work, since it can shed some light on his theory of human behaviour, as well as reminding us of the influence of the French freethinking tradition upon his thought.[1]

Bayle, his great predecessor, had two articles in his dictionary on the subject. He said, rather laconically:

"I hope they will occasion the clearing of a subject, hwich is not less difficult than important."[2] We shall see how this in fact manet that Bayle would try to dispel the 'strange doctrine' that animals were mere automata.[3]

Mandeville's own first recorded views on the subject appear in a thesis which he presented at Leiden, where he was attending courses in philosophy as well as medicine. In the thesis, presented in 1689, he emphatically defends the Cartesian contention that, in fact, animals are mere automata, stating the principle:

"Bestias nulla cogitatione praditas, omnesque illarum actiones automaticas esse".[4]

His attack upon the Gassendist-Bayle position centred mainly on his accusation that they based their case on a false analogy between the behaviour of animals and that of men. Typical of this analogising is using the case of the behaviour of bees who elect queens, divide labour among specialists and generally have the making of their cells and the gathering of honey well-organised. Seeing all this evidence of organisation the proponents of the view that animals do have souls immediately conclude that his evidence suggests design whereas, Mandeville tells us:

"apes moventus ut nos, ergo ut nos sentiunt et cogitant, nulla certe".[5]

The reasoning of his opponents' argument is faulty in that just because they see that animals have sense organs and obviously have various other organs hwich perform similar functions to similar organs of the human animal, they therefore assume them to operate in the same way; whereas, in fact, they are not, in the case of animals, directed by a rational intelligence as they are in human beings. Thus animals have mouths and teeth, but they do not speak. The analogy between animal and human behaviour is faulty.

In the remainder of the <u>Disputatio</u>, Mandeville considers the various views which have been put forward on the subject, mainly deriving from classical sources such as Plato, supproting the theory that animals have souls and are not automata. He dismisses them all, re-asserting the Cartesian position that animals are mere automata, remarking as well that this accords with the traditional Christian teaching about the immortality of man's soul.

It is interesting that Mandeville eventually entirely abondoned this position and in his mature works (such as the <u>Fable</u> and <u>Free Thoughts</u>) takes up the Gassendist-Bayle poistion which he so definitely attacked in the earlier <u>Disputatio</u>. Kaye has suggested that his earlier views may have been strongly influenced by the fact that when he presented it at Leiden, Burcherus de Volder was his tutor and he was a Cartesian of such a violent persuasion that eventually the university authorities took steps to stop his onslaughts on Aristotelianism.[6] Mandeville himself refers to the violence of this academic dialectic in his medicat treatise

on the Hypocondriack and Hysterick Passions[7] and de Volder's
tutelage must have had an influence on him. In addition, however,
as Kaye remarks, by the time he came to write his mature works,
Mandeville had extensively read such writers as Bayle and Gassendi,
as well as Fontaine whose Fables he translated as his first
exercise in English in 1703/4. All these writers adopted an anti-
Cartesian position. Most significant of all was the fact that by
this stage he had developed his own theory about the causes of
human behaviour and rather than abandoning the automatism of
animals, he had in fact extended it to include men as well as
animals among the automata. These changes were accompanied by a
development in his libertin tendency, so that the Christian
assumption inherent in his student attitude had completely vanished
in his later writings.

The resemblance between animals and men had in fact been a
commonplace in antiquity. Man was only considered a being sui
generis from Christian times. Freethinkers like Montaigne,
however, defended the kinship of man and beast as did Charron, La
Mothe, Le Vayer as well as Gassendi and Bayle.

Bayle's two articles in the 'Dictionary' devoted to the
subject are 'Pereira' and 'Rorarius'. He ironically introduces the
former by telling us that Pereira was:

"A Spanish physician who lived in the sixteenth century. He
set up for a spirit of contradiction, for he affected to oppose
doctrines that were best established and to maintain paradoxes."[8]

These 'best established' doctrines were those which supported
the theory that animals did feel and think. Descartes, according
to Bayle, was only driven to assert the opposition because
otherwise the entire basis of his philosophy - the mind/body;
thinking extended substances dichotomy - would have been
undermined. Thus he had to oppose

"an opinion which has not only appeared undeniable to everybody but is also attended with an evidence almost invincible."[9]

Bayle does not say at this point what this 'invincible evidence' is, but he goes on to discuss classical views of the subject which on the whole supported his own view that the souls of beasts were different from men only more or less and that animals did think and feel.[10] This is particularly important in regard to Mandeville's theory of human behaviour, as we shall see.

In the remainder of 'Pereira' Bayle satisfies himself that the Cartesian view could not have derived from Aristotle,[11] and promises to return to the subject and give his own opinion in 'Rorarius'.

In this second article, Rorarius, he says in his polemical manner:

'Tis pity that the opinion of Descartes should be so hard to maintain and so far from likelihood for it is otherwise very advantageous to religion, and this is the only reason which hinders some people from quitting it."[12]

Here again he has lighted upon a vital point for contemporaries: if the difference between man and beasts is denied, what are the implications for traditional Christian teaching?

Bayle is not deterred, but he delays coming to any conclusion. He learnedly goes through most of the arguments philosophers have used on this subject, taking time to repudiate those with whom he disagreed.[13] He dismisses the argument that free will is a distinguishing feature of human nature and suggests that existence of a soul by saying that children and madmen have not 'free-will', yet they still have souls. The argument cannot be used to refute the souls of animals. His eventual appeal is to experience and he says that we must conclude from an observation of their behaviour that beasts reason on some say otherwise we could not account for their actions. He enlists the authority of Leibniz and Locke to support his argument.

It is against this background that we must consider Mandeville's mature opinion on the subject. In Part I of the Fable, he relates a fable about a lion ("one of the breed that ranged in Aesop's day") who encounters a shipwrecked merchant in North Africa and asks the merchant to give[14] tolerable reasons why he, the Lion, should not devour him. At first the merchant tries to dissuade the lion by flattery but at length, when this fails to impress the beast, he resorts to the argument that it is evidently absurd that God should have designed men for nothing better than to be eaten by savage beasts when they are so evidently superior to them. The lion asks to know in what way man excels beasts unless it is in the extent of his pride and avarice. The merchant replies that men have rational souls and their superiority consists in their intelligence and feeling. This does not impress the lion who merely takes it as another example of the grossness of human vanity. In his view, men remain puny, fearful of animals who have to huddle together in society,[15] whilst lions are majestic and fearless and worshipped by all other animals. Not only are men weak in the lion's eyes, but they are cruel and vain-glorious as well.

Mandeville ends the discussion at this point by saying that he considers the lion's view of man as being rather extreme, yet it contains some truth. Humans are exceedingly vain creatures and should be moved by the agony that can result from their cruelty, as when a "large and gentle"[16] bullock moans and bellows at its cruel death. With some rhetorical eloquence, he asks:

"When a Creature has given such convincing and undeniable Proofs of the Terrors upon him and the Pain and Agonies he feels, is therre a Follower of Descartes, so inur'd to Blood, as not to refute, by his Commiseration, the Philosophy of that vain Reasoner?"[17]

Later in the second part of the *Fable*, Mandeville returns to the question of comparing men and animals, observing that many creatures have brains and act in response to certain types of emotion etc. When Horatio asks Cleomenes if he doesn't think that horses and dogs can think, Cleomenes replies in the affirmative adding:

"though in a Degree of Perfection far inferior to us."[18]

Further on in the dialogues, he adds that he admires the lion because Nature:

"has not a Machine, of which every Part more visibly answers the End, for which the whole was form'd."[19]

This mechanical model he applies both to animals and human, and a crisis in this heresy is reached in the Third Dialogue of the second part of the *Fable* when Horatio speaks:

"You'll make men as mere machines, as 'Cartes does brutes";

To which Cleomenes replies:

"I have no such Design: but I am of Opinion, that Men find out the use of their limbs by Instinct, as much as Brutes do the use of theirs; and that, without knowing anything of Geometry and Arithmetick, even Children may learn to perform Actions, that seem to bespeak great Skill in Mechanicks and a considerable Depth of Thought and Ingenuity in the Contrivance besides."[20]

In a footnote to this section, Kaye claims that Cleomenes' reply here is an evasion:

"Although Mandeville believed that animals feel and think he none the less held the doctrine that they are automata. What he repudiated is only the Cartesian aspect of the doctrine; Mandeville differed from Descartes in contending, first, that the automata have feelng, and second, that men as well as animals are machines. What Mandeville held was not, "Brutes are like men; therefore they are not automata," but "Brutes are like men; consequently these animal automata feel. In thus refusing to separate men from the animals and declaring the equal automatism of man and brute, Mandeville was in accord with Gassendi ..."[21]

This is interesting and important, as well as illustrating the closeness of Mandeville's opinions on this subject and his general view of human behaviour. With an important qualification, I would support Kaye's view here, although he might have emphasized the heretical implication of Mandeville's attitude in terms of the prevalent Christian view.

That Mandeville held a mechanical view of human behaviour is evidenced throughout the <u>Fable</u> and indeed all his later works. In <u>Free Thoughts</u>, when reflecting on free-will, he observes:

"But when once we reflect on what passes within us, and consider that in making this choice, at least in things of moment, and that are worth observing, we consult our frailties, and re forced in spite of our teeth to chuse, that, which, to our then present inclination, often to our visible detriment, seems to be most eligible. If we reflect on this, I say, our wills shall not seem to be so free, as is commonly imagin'd."

In other words we are not so free because our actions, in a mechanical manner, are directed by our passions and primarily by the passion for the approbation of our fellows or 'pride'.

Mandeville does not rule out the possibility of 'rational' behaviour from men - that is behaviour based on a rational assessment of the situation in relation to a set of principles men might hold. He does not say that man is entirely an intuitive being like the beasts - on occasions he is genuinely capable of acting from motives. What he does say is that this type of behaviour is not usual from men - generally they are content to be lead on by their instincts, they allow the overwhelming passion of 'pride' to drive them on through life. This we need only see from experience of everydaylife - catalogued, if we care to read it, in the Fable of the Bees.

We have thus come to the very central concern of Mandeville's work by way of the question of animal automatism. Man's irrationality is part of his bestial nature. The expectation of the rationalists, that man may behave angelically, is one of the absurdities that arises from accepting the notion that he has a soul.

-151-

APPENDIX III

Some Remarks on Mandeville as Satirist

    Mandeville'es early writing displays considerable concern with the satirical task of laughing at and exposing[1] the prevailing vices and follies of his own society. Indeed the reflexes of the satirist never entirely leave him and we find suggestions of irony even in the title of his last major work <u>The Origin of Honour and the Usefulness of Christianity in War</u>.

    Mandeville's most celebrated and exclusively satirical work is, of course, his hudibrastic verse, the <u>Grumbing Hive</u> where he shows the ruin which follows when the Bees, in Horatian manner,[2] are answered by Jove in their request for a return to the simple life. The moral is that

    "Bare Virtue can't make Nations live
    In Splendor"[3]

    The poem is an attack on those hypocrites whom he sees enjoying the fruits of a prospering society whilst at the same time pleading their commitment to a simple, ascetic ideal. Paradox and fable are employed as literary weapons to expose this inconsistency and maintenance of double standards. Through them Mandeville intends to show:

    'the incompatibility between traditonal moral standards and actual ways of living.'[4]

    The 'actual ways of living' Mandeville held up to ridicule were those of the 'beau monde' or polite society where a man need only conceal, rather than conquer, his passions.[5]

However Mandeville as satirist has his own uniqueness. It has ben said that satire must involve, apart from the exposure of vice, reference to an ideal against which the society satirized is being compared.[6] Satire is thus concerned with encouraging virtue[7] as well as in exposing vice and it must by implication be prescribing a moral order to replace what is seen by its proponents to be the corruption of contemporary society. Mandeville's satire does not involve any such reference. Although he professes many years later, in <u>Dion</u>, to prefer the 'Road that leads to Virtue' rather than the 'Way to Wordly Greatness',[8] he never describes his utopia nor does he tell us how to attain it. His is indeed a case where

'The satirical form enables him to describe, and even to relish, while apparently rejecting.'[9]

Certainly there is evidence to suggest that despite what he said in <u>Dion</u>, Mandeville was well pleased with the advances which had led the world to his own 'polite' age from the dark recesses of savagery.[10]

Mandeville did not therefore intend to reform by way of his satire. He intended to expose hyposcrisy and inconsistency and in doing that, to unfold truths, as he saw them about human nature. In this way, his satirical intentions are linked inextricably to his psychological theories of human behaviour.

The satirical impulse which is so strong in his early works gives way to this serious analysis; the problems we might have with the ambiguous intentions of the satirist, of which he himself was aware,[11] dissolve in the attempt to unravel the undubitable subtlety of the psychologist.

NOTES TO TEXT

Chapter I: The Nature of Man

1. *Origin of Honour*, London, 1732 p. 131.
2. *Ibid*.
3. Mandeville's name has long been associated with Hobbes' on the topics of free-thinking, selfishness and mechanical philosophy. See F. Hutcheson, *An Enquiry Into the Origin of Our Ideas of Beauty and Virtue* (5th Ed.) London 1753, p. 116/7; P. Skelton, *Deism Revealed Or the Attack on Christianity Candidly Reviewed* (2nd Ed.) 1751 see subtitle where both their names are to be found, J. Brown, *Honour a Poem*, 1743 11177/8 where they are described as 'Detested Names'; A. Smith, *Theory of Moral Sentiments*, London, 1759 p. 389 where Mandeville is listed a follower of Hobbes and later in the British Critic, Sept. 1819 NS xii 285-301, in Crabbe *The Critical Heritage* Ed Pollard, London 1972 where they are described as 'selfish and detestable sophists'; L. Stephen, *English Thought in the Eighteenth Century* Harbinger, 1962 2 Vols, Vol II p28 and F. A. Hayek, Dr. Bernard Mandeville, Lecture on a Mastermind, *Proceedings of the British Academy*, Vol III, London 1966 p. 133. Mandeville himself was certainly aware of Hobbes' writings - see *Fable I* p. 179 and II p. 156 for specific references by him to Leviathan and to Hobbes. See also F.S. McNeilly, 'Egoism in Hobbes', *The Philosophical Quarterly*, 1966 Vol. 16 No. 64 where he discusses Hobbes' mechanism.
4. Mandeville recognised that he was portraying the 'meanness and deformity' of human nature rather than its more beautiful features. See *Fable I*, p.5 where he compares himself with Montaigne in this respect and *Dion* p.48 where he tells Berkeley this. Also Bayle of whom it has been said: 'Bayle is concerned not with the elect, but with fallen humanity, and his main concern is to reveal their vices, to show that their virtues are only vain appearance, and that their acts of piety, in fact, mask their true motives which are their base human passions,' W. Rex, *Essays on Pierre Bayle and religious controversy*, M. Nijhoff, The Hague, 1965 p. 57.
5. For seventeenth and eighteenth century discussion of the 'Passions', see A. O. Lovejoy, *Reflections on Human Nature*. Baltimore 1961 p. 161 et seq. For a modern discussion of the philosophical problems arising from the concept of emotion, see E. Bedford, 'Emotions', *Essays in Philosophical Psychology*, (Ed. D.F. Guftafson), Macmillan, Lond, 1961 p. 129 et seq.

6. The characters of Cleomenes and Horatio make their first appearance in Part II of the Fable of the Bees, where Mandeville specifically identifies the former as his spokesman, tho' Horatio also utters opinions Mandeville himself was sympathetic with. See Fable II p. 21 and Kaye's fn 2.
7. For Mandeville, 'Passion' is a term of art which I will show he derives from a single source. Cf. Hobbe's position, M.M. Goldsmith Hobbes's Science of Politics, Columbia P., New York and London, 1966 p. 71.
8. Origin of Honour, p. 31.
9. While recognizing the development in the seriousness of Mandeville's work which takes him beyond the satire of his early writing, the reader should not be insensitive to the continuing importance of his satirical inclinations on the style and mood of later writings (eg. see Dion, his last work).
10. Fable I p. 6.
11. See Preface to Fifteen Sermons by J. Butler (Ed. Matthews), Bell, London 1969 p. 10 where Butler does distinguish them. A modern critic has said that Butler's use of the terms implied the satisfaction of a mental or emotional desire in the case of 'passion' and the satisfaction of a physical desire in the case of 'appetite'. See E.C. Mossner Bishop Butler and the Age of Reason, New York 1936, p. 109. Mandeville uses both words interchangeably, see Fable I p. 142, 344. He also sometimes uses the word 'impulse' and sometimes, referring to 'passion', 'frailty'. See Fable I p. 143; ibid. I p. 139.
12. N. Rosenberg 'Mandeville and Laissez Faire', Journal of the History of Ideas, 1963, Vol XXIV No. 2 p. 187.
13. See M.M. Goldsmith op.cit. p. 51; and infra Chap III.
14. Fable I 281.
15. Ibid 184.
16. Fable I p. 41.
17. For Hobbes, Fable II p. 156, for Temple, Ibid. p. 191 et seq. For Locke, Ibid 190.
18. See esp. Book II, Cap 1. Cf Preface, Fable Ip. 5 where Mandeville says he will consider himself having fared no worse than Montaigne if he gains the latter's reputation for knowing the defects of mankind.
19. See J.S. Spink French Free Thought from Gassendi to Voltaire, London 1960.
20. J.L. 'Abbadie L'Art de Se Connaitre Soy-Meme, Rotterdam, 1692 p. 259.
21. P. Bayle Oeuvres Diverses; 4 Vols, a la Haye, 1727 III p. 87, 89.
22. See L.P. Courtines Bayle's Relation with England and the English, Columbia U.P. New York, 1938 esp. pp8, 141 and 227. Mandeville himself acknowledged his debt to Bayle in the Preface to his Free Thoughts (XV-XVI). Bayle lived and taught in Rotterdam at the same time as Mandeville was at school there; he knew the Rector of Mandeville's own school Jan van

den Bosch and also the Cartesian Professor, Bacherus de Volder, under whose mentorship Mandeville presented his thesis at Leyden University in 1689 on animal automatism. See C. Serrurier Pierre Bayle on Hollande Lausanne 1912 p. 37 and p. 78, and F.B. Kaye in the Introduction to the Fable xviii et seq.
23. A. Pope Epistle to Cobham, Pope: Poetical Works (ed. Davis) O.U.P. London 1966 p. 288.
24. A.O. Lovejoy Reflections on Human Nature, Baltimore 1961, p. 158/9.
25 Ibid. see Lecture IV pp 129-152.
26. eg. Fable I p. 133.
27. Fable I p. 124.
28. Ibid I p. 67.
29. Fable I p. 64.
30. Fable I p. 75.
31. Cf. A.O. Lovejoy, op.cit. 141-144.
32. Eg. 'pride' on p. 108, both of them on p. 112.
33. Fable II 129/130. Kaye is of the opinion that Mandeville's redefinition of the terms arose as a result of Butler's criticisms, which appeared in 1726 between publication of the two parts of the Fable. Kaye proposes three ways in which it is a reply to Butler: firstly, in offering a new word for those, like Mandeville, who call an emotion selfish because they are a man's own; secondly, in affording an explanation of how self-love may dictate an action to one's own disadvange and thirdly, in showing how the emtions and affections Butler distinguishes derive their motive force from self-regard. Kaye's second suggestion seems confusing in that it is self-liking rather than self-love (for even in the old terminology Mandeville would have used 'pride') which may dicate an action to one's own disadvantage. See Kaye's Fn. Fable II 129/130.
34. Horatio later clears this up by saying by saying: 'But what you call Self-Liking is evidently Pride' an opinion confirmed by Cleomenes, Fable II p. 131.
35. Ibid. p. 130
36. Fable II p. 132
37. Origin of Honour pp 6/7 (my italics)
38. See supra. p. 5
39. Origin of Honour p. 12
40. Ibid p. 13 The original contrast of the symptoms is in Part I of the Fable p. 67.
41. See supra. p. 4.
42. J. L'Abbadie, op.cit. p. 263.
43. The distinction continues in the French eighteenth century tradtion being used for example by Rousseau, see Emile, Everyman Edition, London 1963, p. 174. In A Discourse on the Origin of Inequality, Rousseau regards self-love ('self-respect') as a natural feeling while self-liking ('egoism') is a 'purely relative and factitious feeling, which arises in the state of society'. Discourse on the Origin of Inequality, Everyman Edition, London 1963 p. 182 fn.   Voltaire gives an

amusing account of the two types of Self-love, <u>Philosophical Dictionary</u>, Penguin, 1971 p. 35.
44. Indeed it is Butler's crucial response to Hobbes, a subject I shall return to in Chapter IV. See Butler's Eleventh Sermon (which Kaye suggests might have been a reply to Mandeville) <u>Bishop Butler's Ethical Discourses</u> Syllabus Whewell, Ed. J.C. Passmore, Philadelphia, 1855 p. 240 et seq.
45. T. Hobbes <u>Leviathan</u>, Oxford 1909, p. 44.
46. P. Nicole: <u>Discourses</u> trans. by John Locke from Nicole's <u>Essays</u> (Hancock ed.) London, 1828 p. 27 Mandeville mentions Nicole in <u>Free Thoughts</u>, p. 118
47. <u>Female Tatler</u> No 80, January 6-9, 1710.
48. Like Hobbes relying on attraction to pleasure and repulsion from pain. See <u>Leviathan</u>, Part I, Chapter 6. Although some scholars have insisted that this does not entail hedonism on Hobbes' part. See J. Kemp <u>Ethical Naturalism</u>, Macmillan, London p.7.
49. The other remaining passion is 'shame'. 50.<u>Fable</u> I p. 101
51. <u>Fable</u> I p. 100/101
52. <u>Ibid</u>. p. 102
53. <u>Ibid</u>.
54. <u>Fable</u> I p.200/201 Cf Hobbes' definition 'Aversion, with opinion from the object, 'Feare',' <u>op.cit</u> p. 43.
55. <u>Ibid</u>. p. 201
56. <u>Fable</u> I p. 206
57. See <u>Fable</u> II p. 207
58. See <u>Infra</u> Chapter 5
59. <u>Origin of Honour</u> p. 80
60. <u>Tyburn</u> p. 29
61. It can be conquered by a stronger passion, though, as Mandeville discusses in <u>Tyburn</u>, see p. 33 et seq.
62. <u>Fable</u> II p. 207
63. <u>Fable</u> II p. 208
64. <u>Origin of Honour</u> p. 21 et seq.
65. <u>Ibid</u>. p. 24
66. <u>Ibid</u>. p. 23
67. <u>Ibid</u>. p. 19
68. <u>Fable</u> I p. 142
69. <u>Ibid</u>.
70. <u>Ibid</u>.
71. <u>Fable</u> I p. 142
72. Mandeville is using yet another word in addition to passion, appetite, instinct.
73. <u>Fable</u> I p. 142
74. See Note 72.
75. <u>Fable</u> I p. 142/3
76. See <u>Infra</u> Appendix I
77. Success will also depend on an honest recognition of human nature as it is. Thus Mandeville argues in the case of prostitution since it involves a human appetite which will always exist, it is best honestly faced and publicly regulated. See <u>Stews</u>.
78. <u>Fable</u> I p. 202

79. Ibid.
80. Cf Hobbes' definition of anger as 'sudden courage', op.cit. p. 43; & Defoe regarded courage as both a habit and a quality, see M.E. Novak 'Defoe and the Nature of Man', Oxford 1963 p. 147.
81. 'Charity Schools' Fable I p. 254
82. 'Griefe, for the calamity of another, is Pitty; and ariseth from the imagination that the like calamity may befall himselfe; and therefore is called also compassion' Hobbes, op.cit., p. 45. Cf. Butler's criticism op.cit. p. 140 et seq.
83. Fable I p. 56
84. Fable I p. 56
85. Fable I p. 56. Later, in Charity Schools, Mandeville returns to the subject of compassion with a graphic description of someone witnessing the destruction of a young child by a wild beast, still maintaining that it is the making of the agent uneasy that is the essence of pity. See Fable I p. 255. Rousseau later, commenting on this passage, said that Mandeville had show a natural quality that made men more than monsters, but failed to recognize that it stemmed from social virtues. See J.J. Rousseau A Discourse on the Origin of Inequality, Everyman, London 1963 p. 183. Later in 'Charity Schools', Mandeville alludes to the uneasiness caused at the sight of beggars see Fable I p. 258, reminiscent of Aubrey's story of Hobbes, see J. Brief Lives, (Ed. O.L. Dick) London 1958 p. 157.
86. See Chapter 3 infra
87. Fable I p. 134.
88. See supra p. 3
89. Fable I pp 134-147. See also p. 140 where Mandeville refers to classical ostracism as 'Epidemick Envy'.
90. Ibid. p. 140/141
91. Fable I p. 141
92. Ibid.
93. Ibid.
94. Fable I p. 202
95. Pride, uniquely, may be 'played against itself' see Fable II 78/9.
96. Fable I p. 334
97. Ibid. p. 135 Also Fear may be overcome by Anger Fable I p. 205
98. Origin of Honour p. 80
99. I have followed R.S. Peters' definition of 'causal' see The Concept of Motivation RKP, London 1960 p. 12 where he says: To give a causal explanation of an event involves at least showing that other conditions being presumed unchanged a change in one variable is a sufficient condition for a change in another. In the mechanical conception of 'cause' it is also demanded that there should be a spatial and temporal contiguity between the movements involved.'
100. Ibid.
101. Fable II p. 139 (my italics)
102. Fable I p. 54

103. Butler's Tenth Sermon is devoted to the subject of Self-Deceit, being especially alive to the danger that self-love convinces each man that he is morally good. See Butler, op.cit. p. 220 et seq.
104. In Free Thoughts particularly as well as the Fable and the Origin of Honour See Free Thoughts esp. Chapters 2 & 5.
105. Fable II p. 77/78
106. Ibid. p. 79
107. Fable II p. 79/80
108. Mandeville explicitly refers to Bayle's idea of 'this Contradition in the Frame of Man.' See Fable I pp. 167/8 cf. Fable II p. 136, and Female Tale No. 80.
109. Origin of Honouur p. 18
110. See supra p. 3 et seq.
111. Fable I p. 155
112. J.L. Abbadie op.cit. p. 259
113. J. La Placette Nouveaux Essais de Morale, Amsterdam, 1697 p. 28.
114. See C. Vereker Eighteenth Century Optimism, Liverpool U.P. 1967 for an account of the eighteenth century rationalist tradition and also cf with C.L. Becker's view that in many ways Reason was an eighteenth century faith, C.L. Becker The Heavenly City of the Eighteenth Century Philosophers, Yale, 1932.
115. See A.P.D'Entreves Natural Law, Hutchinson, London 1951 esp. Chapter 3. I return to this subject in the next chapter.
116. Montesquieu 'L'esprit des Lois', Oeuvres, 1799 Book I. Cap. 1. nd see P. Hazard: European Thought in the Eighteenth Century, Pelican Ed., London 1965 p. 371 et seq. for a discussion of this phrase.
117. P. Hazard op.cit. p. 73
118. J. Locke An Essay Concerning Human Understanding, London 1747, 13th Edition, Vol. II p. 244.
119. J. Ray The Wisom of God Manifested in the Works of the Creation, Aberdeen 1777, p. 63. F. Hutcheson expresses the same sentiments, in a more secular tone. op.cit. passim.
120. See R. Popkin History of Scepticism from Erasmus to Descartes Harper and Row, New York 1968 and also J.S. Spink, op.cit.
121. For Bayle reference, see supra Note 23. For the general influence of other continental writers, F.B. Kaye's introduction is still the most exhaustive, see Kaye's Introdution Part IV The Background, Fable II p. 21. Rochefoucauld whose opinion of courage he cites approvingly, Fable I p. 213; and St Evremond in a dialogue about the way in which Catholic priests keep their flocks in the dark, Origin of Honour, p. 119 for Montaigne, see Fable II p. 131.
122. G.S. Vichert A Critical Study of the English Works of Bernard Mandeville (1670-1733), PhD Thesis, U. of London, 1964.
123. Fable II p. 164
124. Fable I p. 333
125. See A.F. Chalk Natural Law and the Rise of Ecnomic Individualism, Journal of Political Economy, Vol. 59 pp 332-47 August 1951.

126. C.D. Thorpe Addison's Contribution to Criticism' in The Background of the Battle of the Books R.F. Jones et al., Stanford U.P. 1965 p. 317.
127. Ibid.
128. D. Hume A Treatise of Human Nature, Everyman Edition, London 1964 Vol I p. 6. The other philosophers Hume mentions are Locke, Shaftesbury, Hutcheson and Butler.
129. Another account of this tradition is given in B. Willey The Eighteenth Century Background, Peregrine Books, 1962. See also supra p. 37 n2.
130. Fable I p. 345
131. Fable II p. 247
132. Ibid. p. 247/8
133. See supra p. 38/9
134. Lord Shaftesbury, Characteristics (Of Men, Manners, Opinions and Times) London 1711 Volume II p. 20/1.
135. For example the 'Augustan humanists': Swift, Pope, Johnson, Burke, Gibbon see P. Russel The Rhetorical World of the Augustan Humanists, Oxford, 1965 and the Scottish 'philosophers', Ferguson, Hutcheson, Monboddo, Smith, Reid, Steward and Hume. See G. Bryson Man and Society: The Scottish Enquiry of the Eighteenth Century. Princeton 1945. Often part of the 'constancy' of human nature arose from the belief that all men were 'fallen creaters' since the time of Adam. It is also an assuption implicit in most theories of methodological individualism since Hobbes.
136. Free Thoughts p. 144
137. See supra Note 128
138. Fable II p. 121
139. Sometimes affected by the role or position of people in society, thus the differing affects of avarice on people in different social positions see Fable I p. 349.
140. On this subject see F.A. Hayek, loc.cit.; I shall return to this in the next chapter.
141. Kaye claims that Mandeville's insistence on the non-divine origin of language is original, see Fable II p. 288 n1.
142. Sociability is an important eighteenth century theme I shall return to in the next chapter.
143. 'Man's Understanding, beyond other Animals, contributes to his Sociableness' Fable II p. 300
144. Origin of Honour p. 28
145. Mandeville's understanding of 'education', like many other concepts, is strongly psychological.
146. Fable II p. 192 and 231
147. Ibid. p. 318
148. Of the Stews he says: the chief Design of this Treatise is to promote the general welfare and happiness of mankind' op.cit. p. 1
149. For his own awareness of this, see Dion p. 48
150. By complete contrast with Rousseau who deplored the moral corruption which he associated with 'progress' or social development. See J.J. Rousseau A Discourse on the Origin of Inequality.

Chapter II: Civil Society

1. *Fable* II p.46
2. See *Leviathan*, op. cit. Part I, Cap 13, pp. 94-98 and De Cive, Cap. I *passim*.
3. Used for example by Cumberland, Locke, Rousseau etc
4. *Fable* I p. 4
5. *Fable* I p. 40
6. *Fable* II p. 301
7. *Ibid.* p. 303
8. *Ibid.* p. 128
9. *Ibid.* p.301
10. Mandeville takes up Temple's view of sociability in the Fourth Dialogue of Part II of the Fable, quoting from his *An Essay upon the Origin and Nature of Government* (see Temple, Works, 1720 p. 95 et seq) *Fable* II pp. 191-193.
11. J J Rousseau, *Emile*, Everyman Edition, London 1963 *passim*.
12. See *Female Tatler*, No. 62
13. *Ibid.*
14. *Fable* II p. 267
15. It should be remembered, also, that throughout the eighteenth century, history was thought of as a study of human nature in general rather than a study of detailed and particular events, as in the more modern view of it. As Hume succinctly summarized it: 'Mankind are so much the same, in all times and places, that history informs us of nothing new or strange in this particular. Its chief use is only to discover the constant and universal principles of human nature.' (*Essays*, II, 94, quoted in C L Becker op. cit. p. 95)
16. *Fable* II p. 146
17. Cleomenes mentions the miserable condition of the state of inter-family war which may last 'many ages' *Fable* II p. 267 and Mandeville's insistence on men learning only from experience suggests the gradualness of all his achievement see *Ibid.* p. 142.
18. *Fable* II p. 270
19. *Ibid.* p. 271
20. *Ibid.* p.270-1
21. *Ibid.* p. 267/8. This problem faced Hobbes and it may be said to be a weakness in any theory of contract which attempts to make the contract a pact of consenting egoists, for the consideration of when it will be in their interests not to obey the contract must arise. For a discussion of this subject, see D P Gauthier Ed. *Morality and Rational Self-Interest*, Prentice Hall, New Jersey, 1970 p. 16 et seq.
22. Cf. Mandeville's fiercesome description of a lion *Fable* II p. 233/4.
23. *Ibid.* p. 247
24. See F A Hayek, loc. cit. pp. 139/141
25. See *supra*, Chapter I.
26. See *Fable* II p. 238

27. See Fable II pp. 243/252 for Mandeville's reminder that Man is not at the centre of the universe.
28. Arising, of course, from Aristotle, See Politics Book 1, 2 Works (trans. J A Smith & W D Ross) Vol. X Oxford, 1966 Ed. 1253 where he says: 'Hence it is evident that the state is a creation of nature, and that man is by nature a political animal! cf. Cicero, de Officiis, Everyman Edition, 1909 p. 69 where sociable men are compared with bees.
29. Fable II p. 185
30. Ibid.
31. Ibid. p. 186
32. See Fable I p. 41 & p. 347.
33. Fable II p. 184
34. Creatures without understanding may kill themselves from fear before saving themselves by eating, as birds do Fable II p. 184.
35. Ibid. p. 300
36. Ibid.
37. Fable II p. 300 Man's understanding thereby helps him to satisfy the 'multiplicity of his desires' and to overcome the obstacles in the way of his satisfaction. (See Fable I, p. 344). The view of economic and psychological needs and wants contributing to man's becoming a social creature rather than this being a natural 'instinct' in the Aristotelian manner, is expressed by Mandeville in the Female Tatler, see No. 62.
38. Fable II p. 133
39. Again deriving from Aristotle, Politics (See Book I caps 3-13 op. cit.) this idea was much discussed by seventeenth and eighteenth century social and political theorists, eg. see Sir William Temple, op. cit. p. 101).
40. Fable II p. 201
41. See supra Chapter I.
42. Fable II p. 133/4
43. Ibid. p. 202
44. Ibid.
45. Fable II p. 203
46. See supra. Note 10
47. Fable II p. 242
48. Ibid. p. 261
49. Ibid. p 267 and p. 266 (brackets)
50. Fable II p. 267
51. Ibid.
52. Cf. Hobbes, Philosophical Rudiments Concernign Government and Society, English Works, Sir W Molewsorth, London 1841 Vol. II pp. 2-6.
53. Cleomenes mentions 'three or four' (Ibid. p. 268) but I have already said that we cannot read Mandeville's occasional mention of chronology too literally, see supra. p. 34
54. Fable II p. 268
55. C Darwin mentions in this theory of biological evolution that the struggle for life is most severe between individuals and varieties of the same species. See C Darwin, Origin of Species, Murray, London 1890 Vol. I p. 93.

56. It differs from the other two 'steps' in being a human invention.
57. See *supra*. p. 36 et seq.
58. *Fable* II p. 200
59. See A Ferguson, *An Essay on the History of Civil Society*, 1767 (1966 ed) Edinburgh U.P. p. 122. The passage is also quoted by F A Hayek, *loc. cit.* p. 140 where he considers this tradition.
60. I have considered the account of social evolution in Part II of the *Fable* first although it appeared fifteen years after the account of socialization in Part I, (1714 and 1729 respectively) because logically the later account is properly read as a background to the earlier one. I consider the relations of the two accounts *infra*. p. 47 et seq.
61. *Fable* I p. 42
62. *Ibid*.
63. *Ibid*. p. 43
64. *Fable* I p. 43/4
65. *Ibid*. p. 48/9
66. *Fable* I p. 51
67. *Ibid*. p. 51
68. See *infra* Chapter III where this matter is more fully discussed.
69. Also see *supra* p. 32 on childrens' love of domination and on their 'training' for society.
70. *Fable* I p. 53/4
71. *Ibid*. p. 54
72. Eg. with regard to 'pride' he says: 'in an artful Education we are allow's to place as much Pride as we please in our Dexterity of concealing it.' *Fable* II p. 79.
73. See *supra*. p. 37 on how 'understanding' is useful to man after he has entered society, dangerous before he does so.
74. *Fable* I p. 347/8
75. *Fable* I p. 347
76. *Ibid*. p. 42
77. Maxwell says that Mandeville sharply contrasts the personal and functional aspect of all members of society; politicians have the task of taking the functional veiwpoint. See J C Maxwell, 'Ethics and Politics in Mandeville', *Philosophy* Vol. 26, 1951, pp. 242/52
78. *Fable* II p. 318
79. *Ibid*.
80. *Fable* II p. 319. Mandeville uses the phrase 'dextrous management' in other parts of the work, I.11 and 369. He also uses the adjectives 'cunning' (Ip. 347) and 'skilful' (Ip. 51) to describe political management.
81. See *supra* Chapter I.
82. *Fable* II p. 79
83. I Primer's Introduction to *Fable of the Bees*, Capricorn Ed., New York, 1962 p. 10. Later, however, he adds: 'His later version of the socialization of man did not cancel but rather incorporated the earlier ...' *op. cit*. p. 12.

84. See A O Lovejoy, op. cit. p. 176. A contemporary who did take it very literally asked rather absurdly for the philosopher's name who first discovered the power of flattery, the disputes there were on such an occasion and how long the world had been existing when it happened. See W Law Remarks upon a Late Book, entitled the Fable of the Bees, London 1724 p. 16.
85. I am here talking of 'contract' in terms of his politico-social theory in a general sense. He does, of course, pay lip-service to the notion of a constitutional contract between King and his subjects, mainly to support taking up an anti-Jacobite position. But the whole weight of his psychological and social theory works against the notion of a contract in any philosophical sense.
86. Fable I p. 344
87. The state is for Mandeville the 'body politick' and I have set out above the quotation where he defines it. See supra 46.
88. I consider the question of self-liking and self-interest in the following two chapters.
89. Fable I p. 347
90. F A Hayek says of this kind of theorizing: 'The first thing that should be said is that it is primarily a theory of society, an attempt to understand the forces which determine the social life of man and only in the second instance a set of political maxims derived from that view of society.' F A Hayek, Individualism and Economic Order, London 1949, p. 6.
91. Mandeville considers the traditional Aristotelian typology of constitutions, Monarchy, Aristocracy and Democracy. See Fable I p. 348.
92. Fable I p. 346
93. Part of Mandeville's general scepticism of human nature and human affairs.
94. A Pope 'Essay on Man' Poetical Works (Ed. Davis) O.U.P. London 1966 p. 267. Mandeville's own words are 'All Governments are good alike', Free Thoughts, p. 297.
95. Summarized in Pope's famous aphorism from the Essay, 'Whatever is, is right', op.cit. p. 279.
96. Free Thoughts p. 301
97. Cf. Thompson's description of Britain's 'matchless constitution' A R Humphrey's The Augustan World, Methuen, London 1954 p. 100.
98. See J G A Pocock 'Machiavelli, Harrington and English Political Ideologies in the Eighteenth Century', William and Mary Quarterly 3rd. Series No. 22 1955, pp. 549-583.
99. Mischiefs p. 6
100. Discussing the politics of the Walpole period, Goldsmith says: 'Only occasionally does Mandeville mention subjects that relate unambiguously to the 1720s and 30s.' M M Goldsmith, 'Introduction' to Origin of Honour (2nd Ed.) Cass, London, 1971, p. viii, also p. vii.
101. Origin of Honour p. 139 Cf. Fable II p. 42.
102. Mandeville dedicates a large part of Free Thoughts to attacking religious 'faction' or schism (See Free Thoughts,

esp. Cap. VIII) while making a plea for the national interest as well (See Cap. XII); the latter theme being present in early works such as the Pamphleteers.

103. See J H Plumb, The Growth of Political Stability in England 1675-1725, London, 1969 pp. 133/159.
104. M M Goldsmith, 'Introduction' to the Origin of Honour, (2nd Ed.) Cass, London 1971, p. viii where he says the relationship between Mandeville's views and contemporary political debate 'is indirect if not elliptical'.
105. For discussion of this, see J H Plumb, op.cit.; I Kramnick, Bolingbroke and His Circle, Oxford 1968; and A R Humphreys, op.cit. (esp. Part II pp. 52-58).
106. Ashley says: 'Behind and underlying the world of Pope and Addison was a new world of bourgeois habits and culture, which, still insignificant politically after 1688, was swiftly building itself up into the most powerful force in the nation.' M Ashley, Seventeenth Century England 1603-1714, (3rd Ed.) 1961 p. 236.
107. See Plumb op. cit. Cap. 3.
108. D Defoe 'The True Born Englishman', Part I lines 8-11 quoted in I Kramnick, op. cit. p. 195.
109. I Kramnick, op. cit. p. 203
110. Eg. the various 'Aesop' tracts, A Short Account of the Several Kinds of Societies, London 1700; Ecclesia & Factio: A Dialogue between Bow Steeple Dragon and the Exchange Grasshopper, London 1698: Modern Religion and Ancient Loyalty: A Decline, London 1699, Pecunia Obediunt Omnia, York, 1696 etc.
111. Eg. see Ned Ward, The Character of A Covetous Citizen or a Ready Way to get Riches, London, 1702; The London Spy Compleat (In Eighteen Parts) (3rd Ed.), London 1706 and The History of the London Club or the Citizens Pastime, London 1709. W Law, op. cit., G Berkeley, op. cit., H Fielding, An Enquiry into the Causes of the Late Increase in Robbers etc., London 1751.
112. Mentioned by Berkeley, op, cit. p. 86; H Fielding, op,cit. p. xv and eventually taken up, of course, later in the century in E Gibbon's The Decline and Fall of the Roman Empire.
113. L I Bredvold, 'The Gloom of the Tory Satirists', 1776-1794, in Pope and His Contemporaries, Essays presented to George Sherburn, (Ed. J L Clifford & L A Landa), O.U.P., New York, 1949 p. 10.
114. For Swift's career as a Tory pamphleteer, see R I Cook, Jonathan Swift as a Tory Pamphleteer, University of Washington Press, 1967.
115. See M M Goldsmith, 'Introduction' to The Origin of Honour and the Usefulness of Christianity in War, (2nd ed.) Cass, Lodon 1971 p. ix.
116. J Swift 'The Character of Sir Robert Walpole', Swift, Poetical Works, O.U.P. Londn 1967 p. 487.
117. The Craftsman, No. 291 Saturday, 29 th January, 1732.
118. Kramnick calls Mandeville the 'philosopher of avarice', I Kramnick, op.cit. p. 201 et seq.
119. See Fable II p. 330
120. Fable II, p. 337

121. Ibid. p. 338
122. See Pamphleteers, 1703. Other 'heroe statesmen' of his were Louis XIV whose political expertise he admires in the Eighth Dialogue of the Virgin Unmask'd, p. 178 and Cromwell of whom, although he says he is a ambitious and hypocritical man, he still adds: 'Cromwell was a Man of admirable good sense, and thoroughly well acquainted with Human Nature; he knew the mighty Force of Enthusiasm, and made Use of it accordingly.' Origin of Honour, p. 164. He also mentions the 'vast genius' of Alexander the Great, see Fable II p. 79.
123. Thus Remark Q deals with frugality, while Remarks L & P concern luxury. See Fable I, pp 181-198 and 107-123 and 169-181.
124. Sir William Temple, Observations Upon the United Provinces of the Netherlands, London, 1705 ed. Temple had been ambassador in Holland and this lent authority to his 'observations'.
125. See infra Appendix I for Mandeville's Dutch and medical background.
126. Fable I, p. 187
127. Ibid. p. 185
128. Thus one modern writer has said: 'Financial subjects were first brought prominently into ethical controversy by Mandeville'. J Bonar, Philosophy and Political Economy, 3rd Ed. London 1922, p. 5/6.
129. L Whitney, Primitivism and the Idea of Progress, Baltimore, 1934 p. 45.
130. Fable I, p. 108
131. See Kaye's Introduction, Fable I p. xcvii
132. It has been said that in the eighteenth century, luxury meant firstly commodities not necessary for mere existence (Mandeville's sense), secondly specific products which led to a waste of time, energy, or dissipated morals and thirdly imported commodities which were neither necessary nor productive. See M E Novak, Economics and the Fiction of Daniel Defoe, U. of California Press, Berkeley, 1962 p. 136.
133. Fable I p. 107
134. Ibid. p. 108. Mandeville is aware of the rigour of this definition.
135. On the subject of mercantilism, see E F Heckscher, Mercantilism, (trans. Shapiro) London 1935 where he refers to the Fable as 'exceptionally illuminating' p. 120.
136. Fable I p. 116
137. For a discussion of Mandeville and interventionism, see I Rosenberg, 'Mandeville and Laissez-Faire', Journal of the History of Ideas, 1963 Vol. xxiv, No.2.
138. Fable I p. 169
139. F A Hayek 'Dr Bernard Mandeville', Lecture on a Master Mind, British Academy 1966, p. 134. The passage on the cloth is in Fable I p. 356; the enunciation of the division of labour in Fable II p. 284.
140. Fable I p. 358

141. Mandeville was not supported in this argument by Temple who insists on the effeminacy caused by luxury, see W Temple, <u>An Essay Upon the Origin and Nature of Government</u>, Works, 1720 ed., London, p. 105 et seq. Others who shared Temple's views were A Campbell in <u>An Enquiry Into the Origin of Moral Virtue</u>, 1728, p. 68 where he says: 'we must not weaken and effeminate our minds abd bodies by luxury, softness or delicacy.' R Nelson in <u>An Address to Persons of Quality and Estate</u>, London 1715 p. 9. A foreign visitor to London in the 1720s alludes to 'la debauche extraordinaire qui regne ouvertment à Londres', C de Sausure <u>Lettres et Voyages</u> 1725-29, Lausanne 1903 p. 197.
142. Keynes, himself iconoclastic, comments on Mandeville's heresy amusingly: 'No wonder that such wicked sentiments called down the opprobrium of two centuries of moralists and economists who felt much more virtuous in possession of their austere doctrine that no sound remedy was discoverable except by the utmost of thrift and economy both by the individual and by the state. M Keynes, <u>General Theory of Employment, Interest and Money</u>, London, 1936 p. 362.
143. Voltaire opens his article on luxury in the <u>Philosophical Dictionary</u>, Penguin, London 1971 p. 290 with these words: 'For 2,000 years people have declaimed in verse and prose against luxury, and have always loved it.
144. S Jenyns said 'Luxury maintains its thousands' contending that this supported the notion that -private vices could led to public benefits. S Jenyns, 'A Free Enquiry into the Nature and Origin of Evil', 3rd ed. 1758, in <u>A Guide to British Moralists</u>, (Ed. D H Monro) London 1972 p.229.
145. R Nelson <u>op.cit</u>, p9
146. G Berkeley, <u>op. cit</u>. p. 86 also see <u>supra</u>. Note 112
147. E Rotwein '<u>Introduction</u>' to D Hume 'Of the Refinement in the Arts' <u>Writings on Economics</u>, 1955, p. xcii.
148. <u>Ibid</u>. p. 30. Rotwein also says: 'in speaking of the "libertine" view he (Hume) had most specifically in mind Mandeville's paradox of the <u>Fable of the Bees</u>, where, in his deliberately outraging attack on the traditional rationalist morality, Mandeville had argued that as it stimulated employment, even the most extravagant self-indulgence was socially praiseworthy', <u>Ibid</u>. p. xciii.
149. Ibid. p. 312
150. B Willey, <u>op.cit</u>. p. 98
151. See S Butler, <u>Hudibras</u>, 1663. Mandeville had red '<u>Hudibras</u>' which he mentions, <u>Stews</u> p. 36.
152. Eg. Swift translated or paraphrased many of Rochefoucauld's maxims, eg. see 'The Life and Character of Dean Swift' and 'Verses on the Death of Dr Swift', Swift, <u>Poetical Works</u>, O.U.P., London 1967 pp. 490-513. Mandeville himself quotes a maxim of Rochefoucauld concerned with how vanity and shame are ingredients of courage, <u>Fable</u> I p. 213 and see Kaye's n. <u>Ibid</u>. On this subject also see F Gregoire, <u>Bernard Mandeville et 'La Fable des Abeilles'</u> Nancy, 1947 p. 159 et seq. and L I

Bredvold, loc.cit., p. 5/6. Also see Adam Smith who associated their names: Theory of Moral Sentiments 1759 p. 373.
153. The Modest Proposal appeared in 1729 after the 2nd edition of the Fable (1723) which, with the Essay on Charity and Charity Schools appended and the subsequent action of the Grand Jury of Middlesex in 'presenting' the book, had earned Mandeville notoriety. Kramnick's guess is therefore a plausible one, see I Kramnick, op.cit. p. 231.
154. The Dunciad was written in 1726, dedicated to Swift. Pope talks of Mandeville being able to 'prate no more' and in a footnote refers to him as an 'immoral philospher'. Pope, Poetical Works, O.U.P., London 1967 p. 523.
155. Written in 1733.
156. A Pope, op.cit., p. 306. A similar theme is uttered in Ward's London Spy, (3rd ed.) London, 1706 p. 59 where he says:
 'The Ancient purity you once might boast
  In Interest, Pride, and Flattery now is lost.'
157. This appeared in 1727 and was also dedicated to Swift.
158. Cf. Mandeville's 'Grumbling Hive', Fable I pp. 17-37
159. Gay's Fables span the years 1727-1738. The advertisement to the second volume says that these tables are 'mostly on Subjects of a graver and more political turn' and I therefore refer to them as his 'political' fables to distinguish them from the ones in the first volume which were more purely literary. See J Gay, Fables 1727-38 2 vols. London.
160. J Gay, op.cit. Vol II p- 89-95.
161. For a discussion of this subject, see R F Jones et al., The Background of the Battle of the Books, Stanford, California, 1951.
162. In the 'Battle of the Books', Swift amusingly refers to Aristotle, 'observing Bacon advance with a furious mein ...' J Swift, A Tale of Tub and Other Satires, Everyman, London 1970, p. 160.
163. R F Jones et al., op.cit., p. 18.
164. See infra Appendix I. In the Hypocondriack Passions he says: The real Knowledge we have of nature beyond the Ancients, tht we are not indebted for to observation, would I believe, upon strict examination, not amount to much. Op.cit p. 124.
165. P Fussell, op. cit., p. 84/85
166. Lamprecht says that this puts Mandeville in the ethical school of Aristotle, Spinoza and Hobbes, which sets the achievement of civilized man in contrast to the crude nature of untaught things. See S P Lamprecht, 'The Fable of the Bees', Journal of Philosophy, Vol. XXIII October 1962 p. 562. It certainly contrasts Mandeville with Rousseau: For a comparison of their views expressed in the eighteenth century, see A Smith, A Letter to the Edinburgh Review, 1755, part ii pp. 73/75. An early expression of Mandeville's enthusiasm for civilized life, see Female Tatler No. 62.
167. 'Politeness' of the age was a quality recognised and valued, even if sometimes ironically, by the Augustans. Eg. see J

Swift, <u>Tale of the Tub and Other Satires</u>, Everyman, London 1970 p. 28 where he refers to 'this polite and most accomplished age'. Cf. Lord Shaftesbury <u>A Letter Concerning Enthusiasm</u>, London 1708 eg. p. 16 and Mandeville in <u>Female Tatler</u> No. 98 where he says Tatlers' business is to make a 'civilized and polite society'. Also see P Dixon, <u>The World of Pope's Satires</u>, London 1968 p. 5, and the linking of politeness with happiness and probity: J Forrester, <u>The Polite Philospher</u>, London 1734.

168. <u>Fable</u> I p. 344
169. Otherwise there could be a return to savagery, thus Mandeville's concern with the malfunctioning of the 'system' in <u>Tyburn</u> and the <u>Stews</u>.
170. 'Natural' and 'artificial' harmony of interests is the phrase used by E Halevy, <u>Growth of Philosophical Radicalism</u>. passim.
171. See I Rosenberg, <u>loc.cit</u>. and A F Chalk, <u>loc.cit</u>. for a discussion of the subject of Mandeville and laissez-faire.
175. See C Vereker, <u>op.cit</u>., for a discussion of the complexities of eighteenth century optimism. Mandeville's optimism, as far as it existed, was more what Vereker calls 'empiricist' rather than 'redemptive'. Even in terms of the first category it is restricted and qualified. See C Vereker, <u>Ibid</u>. pp. 107 and 213.
172. A Smith, <u>Theory of Moral Sentiments</u> quoted in O H Taylor, <u>History of Economic Thought</u>, MacGraw Hill, 1960 p. 64.
173. A Schatz, <u>L'Individualism Economique et Social</u>, Paris 1970, p. 77/8
174. See <u>supra</u>. p. 103 n3
175. <u>Ibid</u>.
176. Two mechanical metaphors he uses to illustrate the mechanical nature of society are the clock and the knitting frame. See <u>Fable</u> II pp 323&322. See <u>Sub</u>.
177. <u>Fable</u> II p. 200
178. <u>Fable</u> I p. 369
179. <u>Fable</u> II p. 320/1

Chapter III: Psychological Egoism

1. See <u>supra</u>. Chapter I Note 3. Specifically on their alleged common egoism, see Adam Smith, <u>op.cit.</u>, p. 388/9 and as a modern example H Jensen, <u>Motivation and Moral Sense in Francis Hutcheson's Ethical Theory</u>, Nijhoff, The Hague, 1971 p. 16. An egoistic theory I take to entail 1) that men act only to forward their own self-interest (against the interest of others or the dictates of their conscience and 2) it involves a consciousness on the part of the agent of the reason for his action. See B Gert 'Hobbes and Psychological Egoism' <u>The Journal of the History of Ideas</u> 1967 Vol. XXVIII pp. 503-520 and 'Mechanism and Egoism' <u>The Philosophical Quarterly</u>, 1965 Vol. XV pp. 341-349.
2. Mandeville himself did not use the word 'psychology' nor was it widely used until the 19C. He talks of 'anatomizing' human nature, <u>Fable</u> I p. 145, a term which reminds uf of his medical background, see Appendix I.
3. <u>Fable</u> p. 67
4. See Appendix I. Also of medical theory, see Kaye, <u>Fable</u> I. lxxxvi & I p. 144n & 212n.
5. <u>Fable</u> I p. 67. See also <u>Fable</u> II p. 158/9 for the physical symptoms accompanying laughter. Mandeville also considers Hobbes's comments on laughter; see <u>Fable</u> p. 156/7
6. <u>Fable</u> I p. 211
7. See <u>Fable</u> II p. 122
8. For a brief account of the influence of Locke's sensationalism, see A Chalk, <u>loc. cit.</u>, p. 345. Mandeville's indebtedness to Locke can be seen in his empiricism, political theory and religion as well as in his psychology.
9. <u>Fable</u> II p. 139
10. See <u>Free Thoughts</u> Cap II pp. 25-36 where the characters, Horatio, Emilia and Crato are discussed.
11. <u>Free Thoughts</u>, p. 89
12. <u>Ibid</u>.
13. <u>Fable</u> II p. 139
14. I discuss the subject of determinism <u>infra</u> p. 133 et seq
15. Cf. L I Bredvold, 'The Invention of Ethical Calculus', in <u>The Background of the Battle of the Books</u>, (R F Jones et al), Stanford 1965 p. 169 where he discusses Hobbes's 'new philosophy of motion'.
16. See <u>supra</u> Chapter I
17. <u>Origin of Honour</u> p. 31. The reason why introspection is not undertaken is because of all the acts of 'self-deceit', it 'alone is really mortifying' a does not result in the gratification of any passion. See <u>Fable</u> II p. 79/80.
18. <u>Fable</u> II p. 120
19. See R Peters, <u>op. cit.</u> pp. 12-14 and P Winch, <u>The Idea of a Social Science</u>, Routledge, London 1967 pp. 45-51 where they respectively insist on the need to analyse human behaviour in terms of motives as well as causes. See <u>infra</u> p. 157 n1

20. Fable I p. 55
21. Mandeville considers the behaviour of 'men of honour' particularly in the Female Tatler (Nos. 77, 78, 80 & 84), in the Fable I, Remark R, pp. 198-223, and throughout the Origin of Honour. The existence of this sort of code is an indication of the extent to which English society at this time still retained aristocratic 'manners', see K Thomas, 'Social Origins of Hobbes Political Thought' in Hobbes Studies, Blackwell, Oxford, 1965 pp. 185-237, particularly p. 193 et seq. for a discussion of this thesis in Hobbes's time.
22. Origin of Honour p. 63 Mandeville's words are that "they seek after opportunities of signalising themselves".
23. Cleomenes stresses that honourable behaviour rests upon the basis of oral tradition rather than written laws. See Fable II p. 83.
24. Origin of Honour p. 7 (my italics)
25. Ibid. p. 8
26. Horatio and Cleomenes also discuss consciousness and memory, see Fable II p. 174.
27. See 'Remark B', Fable I pp. 61-63. Also cf. his analysis of the complex motives, arising from the passions of gratitude, pity and envy experienced by 'gamesters'. Ibid. p. 82.
28. Fable II p. 275
29. J C Maxwell says that they perform a unique role in society, assuming a functional as well as a personal role. Yet the 'functional role' of other groups, such as the merchants I have just considered, is also important. J C Maxwell, loc.cit., p. 252.
30. Thus he talks of men being motivated by the same reasons, whether 'savages or politicians'. Fable I p. 348. On the specific motive for politicians he usually cites their ambition for 'immortal fame' as was the case with Cromwell, Origin of Honour p. 230.
31. Origin of Honour p. 35/6
32. See Female Tatler No. 80, the views of the 'Oxford gentleman.'
33. Female Tatler No. 80
34. Origin of Honour p. 3
35. Fable I, p. 124. See supra p. 68 et seq.
36. Origin of Honour p. 6
37. T Hobbes, Leviathan Oxford, 1909, pp. 46/7. Hobbes's words are: 'Will is ... the last Appetite in Deliberating.'
38. See Fable I p. 348. One may note that egoism does not necessarily entail hedonism nor vice versa.
39. T Hobbes, Leviathan p. 47
40. Free Thoughts p. 89
41. Origin of Honour p. 6
42. See supra p. 109 et seq
43. Free Thoughts p. 90
44. See Fable I p. 198-223
45. Fable I p. 120/211
46. I generally use the words 'act' and 'action' where consciousness is involved; 'behaviour' for unreflective actions.

47. Mandevile uses this phrase as a title in the Origin of Honour. See 'The Contents', Origin of Honour.
48. Origin of Honour p. 32
49. Gert points out that there is no logical incompatibility in giving different types of explanation for different types of action. He divides explanations into those of a causal sort, those in terms of motives recognised by the agent, and those in term of 'unconscious motives', the latter, in fact, being a type of causal explanation. (B Gert, 'Hobes, Mechanism, and Egoism', Philosophical Quarterly, 1965 Vol. XV p. 343). Mandeveille does not talk in terms of the latter category, ie. 'unconscious motives' but since in Gert's account they must be understood as causal explanations, it does not matter. He does consider the other two types of explanation as I have shown. Also he interestingly talks sometimes of actions, at one point self-consciously undertaken by the agents and therefore explicable in terms of motives, becoming habitual and unreflective behaviour - thereby being explicable in terms of a causal theory of the passions. This is the case with certain 'mannered' behaviour. See Fable II p. 79.
50. See supra Chapter I
51. Hobbes, Leviathan Cap 6.
52. See supra Chapter I
53. Fable II p. 133
54. L Stephen, English Thought in the Eighteenth Century, Harbinger Ed., London 1962, Vol. II p. 34
55. For a brief but lively account of Mandeville's eclecticism, see B Willey, op.cit., pp. 95-9
56. L Stephen, op.cit., p. 34
57. Ibid., p. 15
58. Fable II p. 301
59. Thus elsewhere, referring to human nature, he uses the words 'rotten and despicable foundation' Fable II p. 64. In Part I of the Fable he speaks of the 'defects of mankind', loc.cit., p. 5. In Dion he talks of the 'meanness and deformity' of human nature, op.cit., p. 48. He also constantly alludes to men's 'frailties' eg. Fable I pp. 42, 139, 208 etc. Origin of Honour pp. 6, 20, 112 etc. Tyburn p. 6.
60. C Vereker, op.cit., p. 10.
61. Fable I p. 324. Mandeville similarly compares himself with Berkeley, see Dion, p. 48. Also see Kaye's Introduction to the Fable lxxii-lxxv and L Stephen, op.cit., Vol. II pp. 52/5 for a discussion of the relationship between Mandeville and Shaftesbury.
62. Fable II p. 178
63. Fable I p. 145
64. See Fable II pp. 62, 73 & 80.
65. To deduce form this that Mandeville's theory of human nature 'can be constructed from the elements of his own character' is perhaps naive and in any case, unsupportable with evidence. See N Wilde, 'Mandeville's Place in English Thought', Mind, 1898, New Series Vol. 7, p. 225.
66. Fable I p. 208

67. *Fable* II p. 208
68. See K R Minogue, 'Hobbes and the Just Man', in *Hobbes and Rousseau*, Anchor Books, New York, 1972 pp.69/70
69. G Bryson, *Man and Society, The Scottish Enquiry of the Eighteenth Century*, Princeton, 1945 p. 23
70. D Hume, *A Treatise of Human Nature*, Everyman Edition, London 1964, Vol. I p 6 & p 5
71. *Ibid*. p. 6 Hume placed Mandeville in the company of Locke, Shaftesbury, Hutecheson and Butler.
72. Cf Willey who talks of the banishment of the supernatural from the eighteenth century, op.cit., p. 11. Also Manuel who says: 'one of the striking expressions of the new scientific and material civilization of Western Europe was an overwhelming tendency to become matter of fact, to eschew wonder, to reduce the fantastic to a commonsense narrative.' F E Manuel, op.cit., p. 26. Similar views are expressed by other writers on the period, thus see P Hazard *European Thought in the Eighteenth Century*, London 1954, p. 30; A R Humphreys, op.cit., p. 180; and L Stephen, op.cit., II p. 2. However the interpretation of this mundanity has been seriously challenged and qualified. See C Becker, op.cit., passim; C Vereker, op.cit., p. 3, F E Manuel, op.cit II p. 6 et seq.
73. *Fable* II p. 229
74. *Free Thoughts* p. 96. Cf Spinoza, who says 'men think themselves free inasmuch as they are conscious of thier volitions and desires, and as they are ignorant of the causes by which they are led to wish and desire they do not even dream of their existence.' B Spinoza, *Ethics* Part I, Appendix, (trans Boyle) London p. 30.
75. *Free Thoughts* p. 98
76. Cf Spinoza: 'There is in mind no absolute or free will, but in the mind is determined for willing this or that by a cause ...' B Spinoza, op.cit., p. 74. Kaye discusses Spinoza's possible influence and mentions Mandeville's one disparaging reference to 'spinosism' in the *Fable* (se I cxi nl and II p. 312 for Mandeville's actual reference) but he does not consider their relationship with regard to the question of free will. Also see *Appendix* II on 'Animal Automatism'.
77. G Cheyne, *Philosophical Principles of Religion, Natural and Revealed*, London 1715 (2nd ed.) p. 138
78. F Gregoire, *Bernard de Mandeville et 'La Fable Des Abeilles'*, Nancy, 1947, p. 33.
79. J S Mill, *A System of Logic*, London 1967 p. 547.
80. A Ferguson, op.cit., p. 140
81. D Hume, An Enquiry Concerning Human Understanding, Section VIII, Part I in *British Moralists 1650-1800*, Ed. D D Raphael, Oxford 1969 Vol. II p. 96/7
82. *Ibid*. p. 97
83. Mandeville's own expression is 'manners and customs may change, but human nature is much the same in all ages.' *Free Thoughts*, p. 144. Also cf Fussell's comments on Locke's psychology implying that every human mind works in the same way. P Fussell, op.cit., p. 55

84. See C B Macpherson, *Political Theory of Possessive Individualism*, Oxford, 1962, pp. 1-100.
85. *Ibid.* p. 61
86. See C B Macpherson, *Political Theory of Possessive Individualism*, Oxford, 1962, p. 54
87. *Ibid.* p. 55. The full eight conditions of 'possessive market society' are: a) There is no authoritative allocation of work, b) There is no authoritative provision of rewards for work, c) There is authoritative definition and enforcement of contracts, d) All individuals seek rationally to maximize their utilities, e) Each individual's capacity to labour is his own property and is alienable, f) Land and resources are owned by individuals and are alienable, g) Some individuals want a higher level of utilities or power than they have, h) Some individuals have more energy, skill or possessions than others. C B Macpherson, *op.cit.*, pp. 53/4.
88. Eg. see K Thomas, 'The Social Origins of Hobbes' Political Thought' *Hobbes Studies*, Blackwell, Oxford, 1965 pp. 185/236 where Thomas depicts the continuance of features of aristocratic society like the code of honour still applicable in early eighteenth century England and assesses the historical evidence against MacPherson's thesis. Also see *supra* Note 22.
89. For the importance of 'coherency' in interpreting a thinker, see W H Greenleaf, 'Hobbes, The Problem of Interpretation' in *Hobbes and Rousseau*, Anchor Books, New York, 1972 pp. 5-36.
90. Thus in *Free Thoughts* Mandeville says: 'Men are naturally selfish, unruly and headstrong creatures, what makes them sociable is their necessity and consciousness of standing in need of each other's help to make life comfortable; and what makes this assistance voluntary and lasting are the gains or profit accruing to individuals for services done to others, which in a well-ordered society enables everybody, who in something or other will be serviceable to the public, to purchase the assistance of others. And as all the conveniences, and chief comforts of life depend, in a great measure, on the labour and service of others, so he that is able to purchase most of them is in the vogue of the world, reckoned the most happy.' *Op.cit.*, p. 254.
91. See *infra*. Appendix I

Chapter IV: Ethics

1. F A Hayek, loc.cit., p. 127
2. See infra p. 91
3. See infra. p. 91/2
4. That is in 'An Enquiry into the Origin of Moral Virtue', preceding the prose 'Remarks' of Part I of the Fable.
5. The Fable was presented to the Grand Jury of Middlesex in 1723 and condemned particularly for its corrupting influence in blurring the distinction between vice and virtue. See Fable I pp. 383/386
6. W Law, op.cit., p1
7. Ibid. p. 6
8. G Bluet An Enquiry whether a General Practice of Virtue tends to the Wealth or Poverty, Benefit or Disadvantage of a People, London 1725, p. 2.
9. J Dennis: Vice and Luxury Publick Mischiefs: or, Remarks on a Book entitled, the Fable of the Bees. 1724, Preface, p. X London.
10. R Fiddes: A General Treatise of Morality, Form'd upon the Principles of Natural Reason Only. With a Preface in Anser to Two Essays lately Published in the Fable of the Bees, London, 1724, Preface, p. XVI.
11. P Skelton: Deism Revealed or the Attack on Christianity candidly Reviewed (in the writings of Herbert, Shaftesbury, Hobbes, Toland, Tindal, Collins, Mandeville, Dodwell, Woolston, Morgan, Chubb & others) London, 1751 (2nd ed.) p. 267.
12. G Berkeley: op.cit p. 79/80
13. Hutcheson says that the phrase may mean: private vices are themselves public benefits; private vices naturally tend, as the direct and necessary means, to produce public happiness; private vices by dextrous management of politicians may turn to public benefits; private vices naturally and necessarily flow from public happiness; private vices will probably flow from public prosperity thro' the present corruption of men. F Hutcheson, Reflections upon Laughter and Remarks on the Fable p. 41/2.
14. Op.cit., p. 53
15. J Dennis, op.cit., p. 1
16. R Nelson, op.cit., p. 9
17. Published in 1714. The second edition was in 1723, despite there having been another one in 1714. See Kaye, 'History of the Text' Fable I p. xxxiii-xxxvi where he discusses this. The 'second edition' of 1723 first contained the 'Essay on Charity Schools'. Dion was Mandeville's last work, appearing in 1732. Also see Kaye's 'Descriptions of Editions' Fable II p. 386/400.
18. Dion p. 38 Cf Kaye, Fable I p. 2 where he discusses the paradox.
19. Dion p. 38.

20. See Kaye's Introduction to the *Fable*, the sections on ethics which I am concerned with here are xxxviii-lxvi and cxx-cxxxiii.
21. M J Scott-Taggart, 'Mandeville: Cynic or Fool' *The Philosophical Quarterly* 1966, Vol. 116 No. 64 pp. 221-32.
22. M J Scott-Taggart suggests that Kaye's interpretation is 'not noticeably different' from the traditional one, tho' in saying that Mandeville never deduced his *reductio ad absurdium* of rigorism 'it provides us with a picture of Mandeville as simply rather a stupid man, rather than an immoral and impudent one.' *Loc.cit*. p. 221 Scott-Taggart's words themselves suggest there is a difference between Kaye's account and those of Mandeville's contemporaries. He is also unfair to Kaye who would surely not devote such a labour as his edition of the *Fable* to the works of a 'stupid man'!
23. M J Scott-Taggart, *loc.cit*., p. 228
24. *Ibid*.
25. *Ibid*.
26. It is also unconvincing in suggesting that Mandeville should not have deduced his practical *reductio ad absurdiium*.
27. M J Scott-Taggart, *loc.cit*., p. 228
28. See J C Maxwell, *loc.cit*., p. 242
29. For an exception, see J Colman, who takes pains to point out that his paper is not concerned with the infamous paradox. J Colman, *loc.cit*., p. 125.
30. Forming Part I of the *Fable*, 1714. See *supra* Note 17 for reference to Kaye's discussion of editions.
31. Eg. cf Ferguson, *op.cit*.
32. A O Lovejoy, *Reflections on Human Nature*, Baltimore, 1968 p. 176
33. *Fable* I p. 42
34. *Ibid*. I p. 47
35. 'The device of the primeval sage or lawgiver deliberately contriving ways to 'civilize mankind' seems to us, of course, an absurd one, and it was effectively ridiculed by some of Mandeville's contemporary critics. But it had a literary tradition behind it, it made the story more amusing, and it served his satirical bent by making the whole affair appear as a kind of trickery played upon the naive savages by 'wary politicians' for purposes of their own. But in fact Mandeville himself, as he elsewhere makes clear, did not take this feature of his account of the genesis of moral virtues seriously; it was merely a literary artifice. The transformation of the amoral beast that man originally was into a being capable of morality was not accomplished all at once through the conscious contrivance of a few 'wise men', but was in reality, Mandeville recognizes, a long and gradual process.' A O Lovejoy, *Reflections on Human Nature* Baltimore, 1961, p. 176.
36. See *supra* Chapter II 37. Thus Mandeville's disagreement with Temple whom, he says, ascribes characteristics of civilized man to savages. See *supra* p. 52/3.
38. *Fable* I p. 48/9

39. *Fable* I p. 56
40. Virtuous actions must therefore be deliberative and before we can judge of the virtuousness of an action, we have to understand the motive of the agent. Cf Aristotle's discussion of the necessity of distinguishing voluntary from involuntary actions 'for those who are studying the nature of virtue'. Aristotle, *Ethica Nicomachea*. Bk III, Works (Ed. Ross) Oxford, 1915, Vol. IX 1109/10.
41. In *Dion* he more explicitly attacks this inconsistency. Eg. see *Dion* pp- 18/19, 22-25. Also cf *Origin of Honour*, p. 38 where he says 'The practice of nominal Christians is perpetually clashing with the theory they profess.
42. *Dion* p. 19 cf *Fable* II p. 106. For pretensions to virtue see *Fable* I, p. 254, 257/8, 265. *Origin of Honour* xxi, Inconsistency of position is emphasized in the *Female Tatler* No. 60 and *Fable* II p. 102.
43. *Dion* p. 19
44. *Fable* p. 42
45. *Fable* II p. 64
46. Vide *Fable* I p. 330
47. *Fable* II p. 223/4
48. *Fable* I p. 51
49. *Fable* II p. 154
50. *Ibid*. p. 134
51. *Ibid*. p. 65
52. *Ibid*.
53. *Ibid*.
54. *Fable* I p. 56
55. For a discussion of the subject of motivation and morality, see T Nagel, *The Possibility of Altruism*, Oxford, 1970 and W K Frankena 'Obligation and Motivation in Recent Moral Philosophy' in *Essays in Moral Philosophy* (Ed. Medlin), Washington, 1958. Nagel makes reference to the traditional controversy between 'internalism and externalism', defining the former as 'the view that the presence of a motivtion for acting morally is guaranteed by the truth of ethical propositions themselves;' and the latter, externalism 'holds ... that the necessary motivation is not supplied by ethical principles and judgements themselves, and that an additional psychological sanction is required to motivate our compliance. Op.cit., p. 7 Mandeville's position is internalist.
56. See *supra* pp. 77 and 83
57. See Kaye, *Fable* I p. 129 n
58. See G P Gauthier, op.cit., and D H Monro (Ed.) *A Guide to the British Moralists* for discussion on this subject.
59. But see B Gert, 'Hobbes and Psychological Egoism' *Journalism of the History of Ideas* 1967 Vol. xxvii p. 503-20, where he denies Hobbes is an egoist and F S McNeilly, 'Egoism in Hobbes', *The Philosophical Quarterly* July 1966 Vol. XVI p. 193-206.
60. Butler, Hume and Adam Smith, whilst keen to refute certain features of egoism, themselves accepted a fairly strong degree of selfishness in human nature.

61. J Butler, Sermon XI, Bishop Butler's Ethical Discourses (Syllabus Whewell) Ed. J C Passmore, Philadelphia, 1855 p. 241.
62. Ibid.
63. See Fable II p. 120 n1
64. J Butler, Sermon XI, Bishop Butler's Ethical Discourses (Syllabus Whewell) Ed. Passmore, Philadelphia, 1855 p. 241.
65. J Butler, Sermon V, Bishop Butler's Ethical Discourses (Syllabus Whewell) (Ed. Passmore), Philadelphia, 1855 p. 141. No doubt 'others' was meant to include Mandeville. See supra Note 57
66. Butler refers to Hobbes's definition in Humane Nature, where he (Hobbes) defines pity as 'imagination or fiction of future calamity to ourselves, proceeding from sense of another man's calamity.' T Hobbes, Humane Nature, or Fundamental Elements of Policy, 2nd ed., London, 1651 p. 98. Cf. Hobbes's definition in Leviathan, where he says: 'Griefe, for the Calamity of another, is Pitty; and ariseth from the imagination that the like calamity may befal himselfe; and therefore is also called Compassion, and in the phrase of this present time a fellow-feeling'. T Hobbes, Leviathan, Oxford 1909 p. 45.
67. J Butler, Sermon V, Bishop Butler's Ethical Discourses (Syllabus Whewell) (Ed. Passmore), Philadelphia, 1855 p. 143.
68. Ibid.
69. Fable I p. 254/5
70. J Butler, Sermon V, Bishop Butler's Ethical Discourses (Syllabus Whewell) (Ed. Passmore), Philadelphia, 1855 p. 143
71. Moreover, whatever the consequences for others, mere indulgence of a passion can never qualify for merit in a moral sense. See his treatment of pity, Fable I p. 56.
72. A further reason for my doing so is that Hutcheson did address himself directly to answering Mandeville, both in his Enquiry Into The Origin of Our Ideas of Beauty and Virtue, and in his Remarks upon the Fable of the Bees, 1750 (see Kaye, Fable II p. 431 where he explains his work first appeared in the form of letters to the Dublin Journal in 1725 and 1726). Hutcheson's position and relationship to Mandeville are discussed by H Jensen, op.cit., and W T Blackstone, Frances Hutcheson and Contemporary Ethical Theory, University of Georgia, Monograph 12, Athens, 1965. Also see A Discourse between David Hume, Robin Clerk and Adam Smith (unpublished manuscript of A Ferguson) Intro. E C Mossner, Journal of the History of Ideas, No. 21, 1960 pp. 222-232-
73. J Jensen, op.cit., p. 18
74. F Hutcheson, An Enquiry into the Origin of our Ideas of Beauty and Vitue, London 1753, p. 159
75. The subtitle states that Hutcheson is defending the principles of Shaftesbury against those of the Fable of the Bees. Of Shaftesbury, Hutcheson rather eloquently says: 'To recommend Lord Shaftesbury's writing to the world, is a very needless attempt. They will be esteemed while any reflection remains

76. F Hutcheson, An Enquiry into the Origin of our Ideas of Beauty and Virtue, London, 1753, Preface XX.
76. F Hutcheson, An Enquiry into the Origin of our Ideas of Beauty and Virtue, London 1753, Preface p,XIV.
77. H Jensen, op.cit., p. 17
78. F Hutcheson, An Essay on the Nature and Conduct of the Passions and Affections and With Illustrations on the Moral Sense, 1742 Ed. (Facsimile Repro.) Florida, 1969 p. 20.
79. Cf Rousseau who says: 'Mandeville well knew that, in spite of all their morality, men would have never been better than monsters, had not nature bestowed on them a sense of compassion, to aid their reason; but he did not see that from this quality alone flow all those social virtues, of which he denied man the possession.' J J Rousseau, A Discourse on the Origin of Inequality, Everyman Edition, London, 1963 p. 183.
80. At times Butler does seem to be implying an utilitarian criterion of an action's goddness depending upon it being conducive to happiness but he nevertheless makes clear in Sermon XII that certain actions must be disapproved regardless of the consequences: 'For there are certain dispositions of mind, and certain actions, which are themselves approved or disapproved by mankind, abstracted from the consideration of their tendency to the happiness or misery of the world; approved or disapproved by reflection, by that principle within, which is the guide of life, the judge of right or wrong'. J Butler, Sermon XII, Bishop Butler's Ethical Discourses (Syllabus Whewell) (Ed. Passmore) Philadelphia, 1855 p. 281. For a discussion of the limits of Butler's utilitarianism, see E Mossner, Bishop Butler and the Age of Reason, New York, 1936 eg. p. 121.
81. W Law, op.cit., p. 39 Cf Berkeley who maintained that because reason was peculiar to man, it was natural to him since what was natural to anything was what made it peculiar to everything else. See Alciphron p. 105.
82. B Franklin's epithet, see Kaye's Introduction, Fable I p. xxix
83. This is Mandeville's own example, see Fable I p. 255/6.
84. See G S Vichert, op.cit., and infra. Chapter V.
85. The phrase 'contradiction in the frame of man' is used by Mandeville, see Fable I p. 168. It is Baylian in tone: 'Que l'homme n' agit pas selon ses principes'. See P Bayle 'A L'occasion de la Comete qui parut au mois de Decembre, MDCLXXX', Oeuvres Diverses, 4 Vol. a la Haye, 1727, Vol. III p. 87.
86. Fable I p. 168
87. See Kaye's Introduction, p. xiviii & Fable I p. 48/9 where Mandeville himself denies vice and virtue. Also see supra p. 97 et seq where I discuss Kaye's interpretations and later, Mandeville's definitions.
88. Origin of Honour p. 5
89. I C Kramnick, op.cit., passim.
90. Mandeville himself says, ironically 'Tho' I have shown the way to Worldly Greatness, I have without Hesitation preferr'd the Road that leads to Virtue.' Dion p. 31.

91. Kaye deals with Mandeville's influence on ethics. *Fable* cxx-cxxxiii and M Goldsmith, *loc.cit*., p. xvii-xviii.

Chapter V: Religion

1. *Free Thoughts*, p. 1
2. Ibid., p. 67
3. Ibid.
4. Ibid., p. 68
5. F E Manuel, op. cit., p. 21
6. Ibid.
7. F B Kaye, 'Introduction to the Fable of the Bees', *Fable* I p. liv.
8. The word is used by Mandeville, see *Fable I* p. 145
9. As well as in *Free Thoughts*, Mandeville avoids discussing this subject in the *Fable*. Cleomenes says: free-will and predestination 'is an inexplicable Mystery, I will never meddle with it.' *Fable* II p. 252.
10. *Free Thoughts* cap. 5, p. 46 et seq.
11. Bayle, Mandeville's influential precursor, became notorious for his anti-clericalism, though it has been pointed out that a good deal of his energy was directed against the authority of Rome rather than against Christianity itself. See W Rex, op.cit., p. 35. Also of Serrurier who says: 'Bayle embrassa la foi catholique avec un enthousiasme jouvenile', showing that at least in his earlier years, his faith was strong. C Serrurier *Pierre Bayle en Hollande*, Lausanne 1912 p. 10.
12. *Free Thoughts* p. 212/3
13. Ibid.
14. *Free Thoughts* p. 228
15. The clergy have the same passions as other men to indulge. All men, given the opportunity, succumb to their urge to dominate others. *Free Thoughts* pp 268 and 222.
16. Cleomenes syas in the *Origin of Honour*: 'No set of People have so artfully play'd upon Mankind as the Church of Rome. In the Use they have made of Scripture, they have consulted all our Frailties; and in their own Interpretations of it, most dextrously adapted themselves to the common Notions of all Multitudes.' These include men's fear of the unknown, which the Church has turned to its own advantage by emphasizing the power of Satan through 'strange stories' 'monstrous fables and 'gross lies' of spirits, witchcraft and apparitions. Op.cit., p. 112/3.
17. *Free Thoughts* p. 20
18. Ibid. p. 127
19. He says: How soon Christians began to deviate from the Primitive Simplicity of their Worship is not easily determin'd, but we have reason to think it was very early ... (Prudentius is mentioned as evidence of the historical time when this may have begun) *Free Thoughts* p. 41
20. *Free Thoughts* p. 38
21. The title of Chapter Two of *Free Thoughts* is 'Of Outward of Devotion'. Op.cit., et seq.
22. *Free Thoughts* pp. 51, 52 et seq.

23. Eg. <u>Origin of Honour</u> where Cleomenes says: 'We both agree that no Nation or large Society can be well govern'd without Religion.' <u>Op.cit.</u>, p. 19 in the <u>Fable</u> he talks of the 'Manner after which Savage Man was broke', that is socialized and made to think of the public good by the examples of his religion. Op.cit., p. 46 and see Kaye's note 1.; in <u>Tyburn</u>, he speaks of 'religion' or 'public spirit' assuaging man's fear of death and making men serve the public rather than private good. Op.cit., p. 30.
24. <u>Origin of Honour</u>, p. 24
25. See <u>Origin of Honour</u> p. 24 where having shown how religion supports men's oaths, he then says that it does not matter greatly the 'nature and the essence' of the God he worships or the matter that this worship must take.
26. Cleomenes says: 'For how unknown soever an invisible Cause, Power or Being may be, that is incomprehensible, this is certain of it, that no clear intelligible Idea can be form'd of it; and that no Figure can describe it.' <u>Origin of Honour</u> p. 23.
27. <u>Free Thoughts</u> p. 80
28. <u>Ibid.</u> p. 89
29. <u>Ibid.</u> p. 90
30. The title of Chapter Three of <u>Free Thoughts</u> is 'Of Rites and Ceremonies of Divine Worship' and it is there that he concentrates upon the subject.
31. <u>Free Thoughts</u> p. 55
32. <u>Ibid</u> p. 63
33. F de Voltaire, <u>Philosophical Dictionary</u>, Penguin ed., London 1971 p.131. When Cleomenes explains the origin of religion in the world 'by miracle'; Horatio retorts: "Obscurum per Obscurius. I don't understand Miracles that break in upon, and subvert the Order of Nature ..." <u>Fable</u> II p. 205/6. This can be taken as Mandeville's own view.
34. <u>Free Thoughts</u> p. 64
35. <u>Fable</u> II p. 207
36. Mandeville uses this phrase in the 'Contents' of the First Dialogue of the <u>Origin of Honour</u>.
37. <u>Fable</u> II p. 211
38. <u>Ibid.</u>, p. 208
39. See <u>Origin of Honour</u>, p. 113 where Mandeville talks of the exploitation of human frailty by the Church. Elsewhere Mandevilles points out that the Ten Commandments and all religious prescriptions and rules were devised to counter the frailties and defects of man. See <u>Fable</u> II p. 271 et seq.
40. For a discussion of this subject which includes Fontenelle and Bayle, see F E Manuel, <u>op.cit</u>.
41. F E Manuel, op.cit., p. 47
42. <u>Free Thoughts</u> p. 149
43. Cleomenes thus refers to the 'true deity' (ie. the Christian God) <u>Fable</u> II p. 207 (Cf <u>Fable</u> I p. 50 where he uses the same phrase). Later in the dialogues, Horatio bates Cleomenes with gullibility in accepting any Christian miralce while

considering pagan ones superstitious. Cleomenes answers are unconvincing and lead us to doubt Mandeville's sincerity. See *Fable* II p. 307 et seq.

44. Serrurier refers to Bayle's psychological preoccupations, op.cit. p. 87; he also adds: 'C'est une chose bien ètrange que Bayle, l'homme le moins passionè qu'on puisse imaginer, ait passè sa vie à etudier les passions chez autrui et leur ait assigne un aussi grande role dans la vie.' *Ibid*.
45. *Free Thoughts*, p. 4. Bayle's paradox appears in the 'A L'Occasion de la Comete qui parut au mois de Decembre, MDCLXXX, *Oeuvres Diverses*, 4 Vols a la Haye, 1727, Vol III p. 56 ii. He also says 'Les idees d'honnetete ne viennent point de la religion.' *loc.cit* p. 110.
46. *Free Thoughts*, p. 4; they are "unable to extricate themselves from the Mazes of Philosophy".
47. *Fable* I p. 167. Also see *supra* p. 33 et seq.
48. Cleomenes says: Nothing is more comfortable to Men, than the Thought that their Enemies are likewise the Enemies of God.' *Origin of Honour*, p. 160.
49. Mandeville's interest in duelling is a long and lasting one. He mentions it in a *Female Tatler*, no. 84, alluding to the fact that by it men put themselves above the law; Horatio and Cleomenes discuss it in the *Fable*, see II p. 83 et seq., he considers the habit favourably in Part I of the *Fable*, p. 219; he returns to the subject in the *Origin of Honour*, tracing attempts to check the practice in France. See p. 63 et seq.
50. *Origin of Honour* p. 42
51. 'Vital motion' is Hobbes' term and is distinguished by him from voluntary motion, the former being the course of the blood, the pulse, breathing etc. See *Leviathan*, Oxford 1909 p. 39.
52. *Fable* I p. 184
53. E J Chiasson, 'Bernard Mandeville: A Reappraisal', *Philological Quarterly*, 1970, Vol. 49, pp. 489-519.
54. *Ibid*. p. 491
55. E J Chiasson, 'Bernard Mandeville: A Reappraisal', *Philological Quarterly*, 1970, Vol. 49 p. 515.
56. *Fable* II p. 297 et seq.
57. *Ibid*. p. 211
58. Chiasson also seems incorrect when he does venture into Mandeville's psychology. Thus he says that Mandeville's view is that reason guides the passions (*loc.cit* p. 500) quoting from a passage where Mandeville is saying that this is the case for men of virtue, who are always few. *Fable* II p. 119.
59. E J Chiasson, *loc.cit*., p. 504n
60. G S Vichert, *loc.cit*., p. 156/6
61. M M Goldsmith, Introduction to the *Origin of Honour* Cass, London, 1871 p. xvii.
62. The grounds of their condemnation were i) *Fable* was blasphemous and denied the trinity; ii) that it denied the government of God in the world; iii) subverted order and discipline, in the Church by attacking the Clergy; iv) that it

contained attacks on the universities, which encouraged libertinism; v) that it said that religion and virtue were prejudicial to society and recommended vice, luxury, avarice and pride for the common good. See Fable I. p. 383-386.

63. This appeared in the London Journal on Saturday, July 27th 1723 and was answered by Mandeville in the same place on August 10th of the same year. The Grand Jury's condemnation, the Letter to Lord C and Mandeville's reply are appended to Part I of the Fable, see 'A Vindication of he Book'; pp. 383-412.
64. Fable I p. 389 and 392. And see Kaye's note ibid. p. 387.
65. Ibid., p. 397
66. J Dennis, Vice & Luxury, Public Mischiefs or Remarks on a Book Entitled the Fable of the Bees, London 1724, Preface, p. xvii.
67. Ibid. In another work, An Essay on Public Spirit, Dennis laments the introduction of 'all manner of foreign customs and foreign luxury' into England and says that there is 'very litle public spirit among us'. Op.cit., London 1711 p. 31. No doubt he considered Mandeville as adding to this decline in public spirit.
68. W Law, op.cit. p. 6
69. Ibid.
70. W Law, op.cit., p. 10
71. Ibid.
72. W Law, op.cit., p. 16
73. Ibid.
74. Fable I p. 42
75. Berkeley's term of ridicule in Alciphron or the Minute Philosopher was intended to emphasize the limitations of his contemporaries and their concentration upon the everyday. They operated at a level suitable to the bandinage of coffee houses but not the serious speculation of philosophers' studies. See Berkeley, op.cit. p. 34/5.
76. G J Warnock, 'Introduction' to Principles of Human Knowledge by G Berkeley, Peregrine, London 1969, p. 16.
77. Ibid. p. 11
78. Mandeville mentions Newton in the Fable II p. 219. So far as all his contemporaries were influenced by Newtonian ideas of 'systems', Mandeville is also; self-consciously talking of his system in the Fable II, p. 75 and looking at the mechanism of man ('A wonderful Machine; Fable II p. 96) as the centre of a 'little World' (Fable II p. 178). See Cap III passim where I discuss the 'new-philosophy' of the post-Newtonian 'social scientists'. An interesting contemporary application of Newton's method to other fields is G Cheyne's Philosophical Principles of Religion, Natural and Revealed, 2 Parts, London 1715. Also see H Pemberton, A View of Sir Isaac Newton's Philosophy, London 1728; Pope's intended epitaph, A Pope, Poetical Works, OVP 1966 p. 651; and for a modern discussion on his methodology, R E Butts & J Davis (Ed.) The Methodological Heritage of Newton, Blackwell, Oxford 1970.
79. Cf. Law op.cit p. 10

80. G Berkeley, *Alciphron or The Minute Philosopher* London 1732 p. 106.
81. *Ibid.* p. 19.
82. *Ibid.*, p. 49
83. Berkeley did not refrain from arguments *ad hominem*, accusing them of personal libertinism. *Op.cit.* p. 99
84. Berkeley says that the example of drunkeness shows the fallacy of the paradox since a healthy man drinks more than a drunkard over his life span and therefore contributes more to the public good by his 'virtues'. *Op.cit.*, p. 80.
85. G Berkeley, *op.cit.*, p. 87
86. Thus Lysicles, representing Mandeville in *Alciphron* says: 'What do you mean by quoting Plato and Seneca. Can you imagine a free thinker is to be influenced by the authority of such old fashioned writers?' *Op.cit.*, p. 85
87. Except for the 'Vindication' appended to later editions of the *Fable*, *Alciphron* was the only work of his critics Mandeville answered in print; his answer to that being *Dion*, 1732. He questions there whether Berkeley had ever read the *Fable*, saying that there is no denial of this in *Alciphron* and offering it as an explanation for so poor a treatment of his work by so distinguished a writer. See *Dion* pp. 5, 7/8.
88. We are told: 'Mandeville highly enjoyed the society and port wine at Lord Macclesfield's table, where he predominated, and was permitted to say or do whatever he chose; his sallies after dinner were witty, but not always restrained by propriety and decorum; and pride and petulance of Radcliffe, a common place topic and *to put a parson in a passion* a favourite amusement.' (my itals) J W Newman, *Lounger's Common-Place Book* 3rd Ed., 1805 ii 307-8, quoted in Kaye, *Fable* I p. xxvi n4.
89. In a letter to Kaye, dated 3rd March 1922, *Fable* II p. 452.
90. See *Fable* I p. 235-8
91. J Viner, *loc.cit.* p. 335.
92. *Dion* p. 31 where he says: 'Tho' I have shown the Way to Wordly Greatness, I have, without Hesitation preferr'd the road that leads to Virtue.'

Chapter VI: Conclusion

1. What is more the Fable has always been the main object of attention and Part I more than any other part. Part II of the Fable, Free Thoughts and the Origin of Honour are far less paradoxical and satirical than the early part of the Fable and neglect of them has tended to contribute to an unbalanced view of Mandeville as a writer.
2. Fable I p. 145
3. Fable I Preface, p. 6 et seq.; Fable II p. 31
4. Free Thoughts p. 11
5. He mentions 'Hypocrites' and 'Christians' who are hypocrites, Origin of Honour pp. 35 and 38.
6. Dion p. 8
7. Fable I p. 145. It is also declared in Fable II p. 18 where he says Cleomenes 'took uncommon pains to search into human Nature.' In Tyburn he talks of a 'curious Observer' p. 35; in Origin of Honour of 'dissection' and 'laying open' of principles, p. 77; in Dion he talks of the Fable being 'a Philosophical Disquisition into the Force of the Passions.' p. 54/5.
8. Origin of Honour p. 6
9. See S Lukes Methodological Individualism Reconsidered, in Sociological Theory and Philosophical Analysis, London 1970. (Ed. D Emmet and A MacIntyre)
10. Also see Gregoire, op.cit. p. vii
11. See F A Hayek, loc.cit.; and J S Slotkin, Readings in Early Anthropology, Chicago, 1965.
12. Eg. see Gide and Rist, History of Economic Doctrines p. 72, London, 1948.
13. J C Maxwell, loc.cit.
14. L Schneider, 'Mandeville as a forerunner of Modern Sociology'. Journal of the History of the Behavioural Sciences 1970 pp. 219-50.
15. G S Vichert, loc.cit.
16. L I Bredvold, The Gloom of the Tory Satirists in Pope and His Contemporaries, (Ed. J L Clifford and L A Landa), Oxford 1949, p. 6.
17. D Hume, A Treatise of Human Nature, Everyman, London 1964 Vol. I p. 6.

NOTES TO APPENDICES

Appendix I

1. I have not seen it necessary to include a full biography of Mandeville since this is adequately done in Kaye's Introduction to the Fable I, xvii-xxxii, and G S Vichert's work loc.cit Chapter I. A few new details which I have learnt appear in a letter to me which I sent out infra p. 222 nl.
2. B Mandeville: A Treatise on the Hypocondriack and Hysterick Passions 1711 (Ed. of 1730, enlarged by the author, used).
3. B Mandeville: Fable I p. 20
4. In Fontaine's fable the patient dies as the two doctors called to treat him discuss the cures. He concludes: "L'un disait: "Il est mort; je l'avais bien prevu." "S'il m'eut cru, disait l'autre, il serait plein de vie." Fables Chosies Paris p. 219.
5. See B Mandeville: Aesop Dress'd or a Collection of Fables Writ in Familiar Verse 1704. (Augustan Society Reprint, No. 120 1966).
6. F B Kaye's Introduction Fable I p. xix. Also Geneology Fable II p. 378-385.
7. In a letter dated October 12, 1970. addressed to me from Dr Luyendijk-Eishout of the National Museum for the History of Science, Leiden, is the following information: Bernard came to Leiden on September 17th, 1686, he told the Board that he was 20 years of age and that he wanted to be registered as a student of philosophy (not in medicine!) He found himself a room in the Nieuwsteeg. His landlady was called Neeltje van der See. The next year on February 13th he got himself his permission for tax free beear and wine. This can be read from the so-called "recentie" list. He resided still with the same landlady, according to this list. In 1688 he appears again in the list. This time he resides in the Papegracht, but still with Neeltje van der See. In 1689, the list says that Bernard de Mandeville now stays with Christoffel Preson, on the Garenmarket. This address appears again in 1690, but Bernard has not been registered in February to get his taxfree beer. This means that he may have left Leiden in this year. He is no longer registered in 1691, but he got himself reregistered in the Album Inscriptionum of the University on March 19th, 1691. He gives his address: "apud ... van den Brande op de Breedestraat". (Arch, Sen, 12) and mentions his age 20 years! On March 30th he defended his thesis "De Chylosi vitiata". (in Sen. Med.) This means that the thesis was medical. I do not know when he changed his study into medicine. Christoffel Preston is not a dutch name. There was a 25 years old english

student by that name registered in 1628 in the faculty of theology. It is hardly possible that this young man stayed in Leiden and lived there as a landlord? In 1689 he would have been 86 years old!

8. B Mandeville: Disputatio Medical Inauguralis de Chysoli Vitiata 1691
9. On this subject see K Dewhurst: John Locke, Physician and Philosopher: A Medical Biography London 1963." Especially such as: "Sylvius or Francis de la Boe (1614-72) was a leading iatrochemist who studied fermentation and the nature of the juices of the body. His treatment was directed towards adjusting the acidity or alkalinity of the internal secretions on the principle of contraria contraris. He first described the Sylivian fissure and was an able clinician." Op.cit p. 92 Locke's own opinion was: "Purgatives are bad for hypocondriacs and bring on paroxyms; they spoil the stomach's fermentation, drain off too much of the bile and pancreatic fluid and completely upset the primary process of digestion - hence the sypmptoms of hypocondria." Op.cit p. 247/8-
10. See R J White The Anti-Philosophers London 1970, who says that later in eighteenth century: "Little wonder that he (La Mettrie) now thought it wise to 'expatriate' hmself to Leiden. The university there ... was the most modern and highly respected in Europe." Op.cit. p. 76
11. B Mandeville: Hypocondriack and Hysterick Passions, p. xiii
12. Ibid. p. 60
13. Ibid. p. 33
14. On the subject of hypothesis, Mandeville draws this amusing and instructive sketch in the Treatise: "An hypothesis, when once it has been a little while established, becomes like a sovereign, and receives the same homage and respect from its vassals, as if it were the truth itself: This continues till experience or envy discovers a flaw in it. Yet unless it be a great man indeed, that finds fault first, his discovery is only answered with contempt for a while: But when another hypothesis is broached, which is commonly soon after, that not having the fault of the former and being likewise well contrived, gets a considerable number of followers: The you will see all that fought under the banner of the old hypothesis bristle up, and every man of note among them thinks himself personally injured, and in honour obliged to stand by it with his life and fortune. Now all Arts and Sciences are ransacked, and whatever can be drawn from with, Eloquence or Learning, is produced to maintain their own liege hypothesis, and destroy the upstart one; and the whole party is alarmed with as much concern as they are in a man of war when they have received a shot underwater: In the meantime, they that have lifted themselves under the new hypothesis are not idle and thus both parties enter into a perfect state of war, the better sort fighting with arguments, the rest with personal reflections. This play is generally continued for a considerable time with a great deal of violence ..." Op.cit p. 125/6

15. *Ibid* p. 98
16. He adds: "Tis certainly Pride, that makes them so fond of the Idol, Reason". *op.cit* p. 62
17. *Op.cit* p. 175. Mandeville is careful not to criticize Newton as such, his concern is only to criticize what he considered a bogus and superficial attempt to cloak medicine in Newtonianism, thus he says in the Treatise: "A man of wit and good parts, that has a smattering Newtonian philosophy is seldom at a loss now, to solve almost any phenomena." *op.cit* p. 182.
18. *Ibid.* p. 132/3
19. *Op.cit* p. 233
20. On this also see *Female Tatler* no 66 by Mandeville where he is even more outspoken in support of the apothecaries, and after a tirade against the teaching of medicine in the universities adds: "... every apothecary, who by his trade needs to know no more than the simples when he uses them, and Latin enough to understand the directions how to cook them as soon as he is out of his time, will tell you, that he can do the same (as a physician) without all that heathen knowledge." *Female Tatler* No. 66 1709.
21. K Dewhurst *op.cit* p. 305
22. W L Letwin *Origin of Scientific Economics* London 1963, p. 152
23. *Hypocondriack and Hysterick Passions* p. 351/2
24. *Ibid* p. 63

Appendix II

1. He admits Bayle's influence; Free Thoughts p. xv/xvi
2. P Bayle: A Critical & Historical Dictionary, London 1710 Vol. IV p. 2609
3. Ibid. p. 2515
4. B Mandeville: 'Disputatio Philosophica de Brutorum Operationibus' Leiden, 1689. Mandeville re-asserted this opinion in the corollaries to his doctoral thesis: "Bruta non sentiunt". B Mandeville: 'Disputatio Medical Inauguralis de Chyliosi Vitiata' 1691.
5. B Mandeville: 'Disputatio Philosophica de Brutorum Operationibus' 1689
6. F B Kaye 'Introduction' Fable I, p. cvi
7. Hypocondriack and Hysterick Passions p. 115
8. P Bayle: op.cit. p. 2513; and for Bayle's polemical style and his influence on Mandeville, see Beller & Lee's 'Introduction' to Selections from Bayle's Dictionary, Princeton, 1952; though they comment: "Mandeville certainly pushed Bayle's techniques and arguments fruther than Bayle would have wished." op.cit. p. xxix.
9. P Bayle: op.cit. p. 2515
10. Anaxagoras, for example, Bayle tells us: "placed the difference in this viz. that men are able to explain their reasons whereas beasts cannot explain theirs". P Bayle: op.cit. p. 2516
11. Bayle tells us that Aristotle knew the mechanical power which Nature exercises in the bodies of animals and was not convinced that matter could think; nevertheless he believed animals could feel. Op.cit. 'Note H'.
12. Ibid. p. 2604
13. "The philosophers of the Schools are very much mistaken, if by rejecting that (ie. the rationality of the souls of beasts) they persuade themselves that they shall avoid the ill consequence of the opinion that gives beasts a sensitive soul. These gentlemen want neither distinctions, nor exceptions, nor boldness to decide that the acts of the soul do not exceed certain bounds, which they prescribe; but all this confused and impenetrable talk signifies nothing toward the establishing of a specific difference between the souls of men and beasts, it is scarce probable, they can invent a better explication that what they have given hitherto." Ibid. p. 2606.
14. Fable I p. 176/181
15. Kaye observes that Mandeville may have been alluding to the frontpiece of Leviathan (ed. 1651) showing the picture of a colossus formed of minute human figures. Fable I p. 179 n1.
16. Fable I p. 180
17. Ibid. p. 181
18. Fable II p. 166
19. Ibid. p. 233

20. Fable II p. 139/140
21. Ibid. See Footnote 1
22. Free Thooughts p. 96

Appendix III

1. Mandeville uses the words himself, *Fable* II p. 102
2. Horace, *The Collected Works*, Everyman, London 1961 p. 139
3. *Fable* I p. 37
4. B Willey, *The Eighteenth Century Background* Peregrine, London 1962 p. 99
5. *Fable* I p. 72. Also see 'Preface' to Part II of the *Fable* eg. p. 11 where he discusses the predelictions of the beau monde.
6. B Willey, *The Eighteenth Century Background*, Peregrine, London p. 100 where Willey is quoting from Middleton Murray, *The Problem of Style* p. 65.
7. See Appendix V 'On Histriography and Satire in the Early Eighteenth Century' in C J Parsons, *Swifts Works 1710-15 and Contemporary Ideas of History and Histriography* Ph.D. Thesis, University of London 1968.
8. *Dion* p. 31
9. E Lucie-Smith, Introduction to the Penguin Book of Satirical Verse, London 1967 p. 24
10. Eg. See *Female Tatler* No. 62.
11. Horatio remarks: "But who knows what to make of a Man, who recommends a thing seriously on one Page, and ridicules it on the next". *Fable* II p. 102

BIBLIOGRAPHY

PART I: MANDEVILLE'S WORKS

Bernardi a Mandeville de Medicina Oratio Scholastica.[1] Rotterdam 1685

Disputatio Philosophica de Brutorum Operationibus. Leyden.[1] 1689

Disputatio Medica Inauguralis de Chylosi Vitiata, Leyden.[1] 1691

Some Fables after the Easie and Familiar Method of Monsieur de la Fontaine 1703

Aesop Dress'd or a collection of Fables Writ in Familiar Verse.[2] 1704

Pamphleteers 1704

Typhon: or the Wars between the Gods and Giants: a Burlesque Poem in Imitation of the Comical Mons. Scarron. 1704

The Grumbling Hive: or, Knaves Turn'd Honest. 1705

The Virgin Unmask'd: or, Female Dialogues betwixt an Elderly Maiden Lady, and her Niece. 1709

Female Tatlers[3] 1709/10

A Treatise of the Hypocondriack and Hysterick Passions.[7] 1711

Wishes to a Godson, with Other Miscellany Poems by B.M. 1712

The Mischiefs that ought Justly to be apprehended from a Whig Government. 1714

The Fable of the Bees.[4] 1714

Free Thoughts on Religion, the Church, and National Happiness. 1720

A Modest Defence of Publick Stews. 1724

An Enquiry into the Causes of the Frequent Executions at Tyburn. 1725

Letter published in the British Journal for 25 April and 1 May 1725

The Fable of the Bees. Part II 1729

An Enquiry into the Origin of Honour, and the Usefulness of Christianity in War.[5] 1732

A Letter to Dion, Occasion'd by his Book Call'd Aciphron.[6] 1732

NOTES

1. Paradoxically all Mandeville's works are in English except these three Latin treatises. He has no known works in Dutch.

2. I have used the Augustan Reprint Society (No. 120) 1966 Ed. introduced J S Shea.

3. The Female Tatlers ran fron No. 1, July 8th 1709 to No. 115, 31 March 1710. I have quoted the numbers of them only in the text. Mandeville's contribution in the Lucinda - Artesia papers. I have used the Oxford copy and the following numbers are Mandeville's:

1. No. 52: November 2 to November 4 1709: Lucinda
2. No. 58: November 16 to November 18 1709: Artesia
3. No. 60: November 21 to November 23 1709: Lucinda
4. No. 62: November 25 to November 28 1709: Artesia
5. No. 64: November 30 to December 2 1709: Lucinda
6. No. 66: December 5 to December 7 1709: Artesia
7. No. 68: December 9 to December 12 1709: Lucinda
8. No. 70: December 14 to December 16 1709: Artesia
9. No. 72: December 19 to December 21 1709: Lucinda
10. No. 74: December 23 to December 26 1709: Artesia
11. No. 76: December 28 to December 30 1709: Lucinda
12. No. 77: December 30 to January 2 1710: Artesia
13. No. 78: January 2 to January 4 1710: Lucinda
14. No. 80: January 6 to January 9 1710: Artesia
15. No. 81: January 9 to January 11 1710: Lucinda
16. No. 84: January 16 to January 18 1710: Artesia
17. No. 86: January 20 to January 23 1710: Lucinda
18. No. 88: January 25 to January 27 1710: Artesia
19. No. 90*: January 30 to February 1 1710: Lucinda
20. No. 92: February 3 to February 6 1710: Artesia
21. No. 94: February 8 to February 10 1710: Lucinda
22. No. 96: February 13 to February 16 1710: Artesia
23. No. 98: February 17 to February 20 1710: Lucinda
24. No. 100: February 22 to February 24 1710: Artesia
25. No. 102: February 27 to March 1 1710: Lucinda
26. No. 104: March 3 to March 6 1710: Artesia
27. No. 106: March 8 to March 10 1710: Lucinda
28. No. 108: March 13 to March 15 1710: Artesia
29. No. 110: March 17 to March 20 1710: Lucinda
30. No. 112: March 22 to March 24 1710: Artesia
31. No. 115: March 20 to March 31 1710: Lucinda

* The numbers of the Oxford Female Tatlers which I have used are corrected after No. 89, that being one of Emilia's. I give only the corrected numbers.

4. I have used F B Kaye's authoritative editon of 1924 as my standard reference for this work. I have also consulted the original editions of 1714 and 1729; the French edition of 1740; I have used Primer's abridged Edition (Capricorn New York 1962) and P Hart's abridged Penguin Edition (London 1970).

5.   I have used M M Goldsmith's Edition (Cass, London 1971) as well as the first edition of 1732.

6.   I haveused B Dobree's Edition (Liverpool Unviversity Press 1954) as well as the original edition of 1732.

7.   I have also used 1720 enlarged edition in which the title had been changed from <u>Passions</u> to <u>Diseases</u>.

BIBLIOGRAPHY

PART II: EIGHTEENTH CENTURY AND EARLIER

L'Abbadie, J. : L'Art de se connoitre soy meme Rotterdam 1692

L'Abbadie, J. : Art of Knowing Oneself, Oxford 1698

Aesop : The Fables of Aesop (trans. S. Croxall and R. L'Estrange) London, 1864

Anon : Aesop at Bathe, Or a Few Select Fables in Verse, By a Person of Quality, London 1698

Anon : Aesop at Court, London 1702

Anon : A Short Account of Several Kinds of Societies etc and Other Tracts, London 1700(?)

Anon : Old Aesop at Whitehall, Giving Advice to Young Aesop at Tunbridge and Bathe, London 1698

Anon : Ecclesia & Factio: A Dialogue between Bow Steeple Dragon and the Exchange Grasshopper, London 1698

Anon : Modern Religion and Ancient Loyalty, A Dialogue, London 1699

Anon : Pecunia Obediunt Omnia: Money Does Master All Things, York 1696

Anon : The Insinuating Bawd: And the Repenting Harlot Written by a Whore at Tunbridge and dedicated to a Bawd at Bath, London 1700

Aristotle : Works, O.U.P. (Ed. W D Ross) 12 Vols. Oxford 1966

Aubrey J. : Brief Lives, (Ed. O L Dick) Secker & Warburg, London 1971

Bayle P. : <u>Oeuvres Diverses</u>, 4 Vols, à la Haye, 1727

Bayle P. : <u>An Historical and Critical Dictionary</u> (English Ed) 4 Vols. London 1710

Bentley R. : <u>The Folly of Atheism, and what is now called Deism, even with respect to the present life</u>, London 1692

Berkeley G. : <u>Alciphron: or, the Minute Philosopher. In Seven Dialogues, Containing An Apology for the Christian Religion against those who are called Free Thinkers</u>, 2 Vols. London 1732

Bernard J F : <u>Reflexiones Morales: Satiriques & Comiques sur les moeurs de notre siecle</u>, Cologne 1711

Bluet G : <u>An Enquiry Whether a General Prctice of Virtue tends to Wealth or Poverty, Benefit or Disadvantage of a People?</u> London 1725

Burnett T. : <u>The Sacred Theory of the Earth</u>, 2 Vols. (4th Ed.) London 1719

Butler J. : <u>The Analogy of Religion Natural and Revealed to the Constitution and Course of Nature</u> London 1736

Butler J. : <u>Bishop Butler's Ethical Discourses</u> (Syllabus Dr. Whewell) (Ed. J C Passmore) 1855

Butler S. : <u>Hudibras</u> (Ed. H Bohm) London 1859

Boswell J. : <u>Life of Dr Samual Johnson LL.D.</u> Everyman Ed. 1949

Brown J. : <u>Essays on the Characteristics</u> London 1751

Brown J. : <u>Honour, A Poem</u> London 1743

Campbell A. : <u>Aretelogia or An Enquiry into the Original of Moral Virtue</u> London 1728

Cheyne G.   : Philosophical Principles of Religion Natural and Revealed (2 Parts) (2nd edn) London 1715

Cheyne G.   : The English Malady or a Treatise of Nervous Disease of All Kinds   London 1734

Cicero   : The Offices   Everyman Ed.   London 1909

Collins A.   : A Discourse of Free Thinking, occasioned by the Rise and Growth of a sect called Free-Thinkers   London 1713

Dennis J.   : Essay upon Public Spirit, being a satire in prose upon the manners and luxury of the times, the chief source of our present parties and divisions   Lndon 1711

Dennis J.   : Vice and Luxury, Publick Mischiefs: or Remarks on a Book entitled the Fable of the Bees   London 1724

Defoe D.   : An Essay upon Projects   London 1698

Defoe D.   : A Tour Through the Whole Islands of Great Britain 1724-6   (Everyman Ed.)   London 1962

Defoe D.   : The Life and Strange Surprising Adventures of Robinson Crusoe, 2 Parts, London 1719, and Serious Reflections during the Life and Surprising Adventures of Robinson Crusoe Part 3, London 1720

Defoe D.   : Some Considerations upon Street Walkers, with a Proposal for lessening the present number of them   London 1726

Eachard J.   : Mr Hobbes' State of Nature, Considered, in a Dialogue between Philantus & Timothy   London 1692

Ferguson A.   : An Essay on the History of Civil Society   1767 (Edinburgh Facsimile Ed)   1966

Fiddes R.   : A General Treatise of Morality, Form'd upon the
                     Principles of Natural Reason Only 1724

Fielding H.   : An Enquiry into the Causes of Late Increases of
                     Robbers etc London 1751

Fielding H.   : Jonathan Wild and A Voyage to Lisbon
                     Everyman Ed. London 1973

Fielding H.   : The History of Tom Jones, A Foundling London 1955

Fontaine La   : Fables, Choises Paris 1668

Forrester J.   : The Polite Philosopher London 1734

Gay J.   : 'Beggar's Opera': Eighteenth Century Plays Ed. J
                     Hampden, London 1970

Gay J.   : Fables 1727-38 2 Vols. London

Gay J.   : Trivia or the Art of Walking the Streets of London
                     London 1727

Gibbon E.   : Memoirs of the Life and Writing of Edward Gibbon
                     2 Vols. London 1827

Hale M.   : The Primitive Origination of Mankind London 1677

Hawkins, Sir John : The Life of Samuel Johnson LL.D. London 1787

Hobbes T.   : The English Works of Thomas Hobbes of Malmesbury
                     (Sir W Molesworth) 11 Vols. London 1839-45

Hobbes T.   : Leviathan O.U.P. (Ed. W G Pogson-Smith) Oxford
                     1909

Hobbes T.   : Humane Nature or Fundamental Elements of Policy
                     2nd Ed. London 1651

Hervey, Lord J. : Some Remarks on the Minute Philosophers in a Letter from a Country Clergyman to his friend in London London 1732

d'Holbach, Baron : La Morale Universelle, ou les Devoirs de l'Homme 3 Vols. Paris 1820

Horace : The Collected Works of Horace, Everyman Ed. (trans. Lord Dunsancy & M Oakley) London 1961

Hume D. : A Treatise of Human Nature Everyman Ed. 2 Vols. London 1964

Hume D. : Two Letters to Frances Hutcheson in Selby Bigge (Ed. D D Rahael) British Moralists, 2 Vols. Oxford 1969

Hume D. : Writings on Econmomics (Ed. E Rotwein) 1955

Hutcheson F. : An Enquiry into the Original of our Ideas of Beauty and Virtue (5th Ed.) London 1753

Hutcheson F. : An Essay on the Nature and Conduct of the Passions and Affections, with Illustrations on the Moral Sense (Facsimile Reproduction) Florida 1969

Hutcheson F. : Reflections upon Laughter and Remarks upon the Fable of the Bees Glasgow 1750

Jenyns S. : A Free Enquiry into the Nature and Origin of Evil London 1757

Law W. : Remarks upon a Late Book, entitled The Fable of Bees London 1844

La Placette J. de : Dissertions sur Divers sujets de Morale et de Theologie Amsterdam 1704

La Placette J. de : Nouveaux Essais de Morale Amsterdam 1697

La Rochefoucauld F. de : <u>Maxims</u> Penguin ed. (Ed. Tancock) 1959

Leng J. : <u>A Sermon to the Societies for Reformation of Manners at St Mary Le Bow on 29 December 1718</u> London 1719

Leslie C. : <u>A Short and Easie Method with the Deists</u> London 1777

Locke J. : <u>An Essay Concerning Human Understanding</u> (13 ed.) 2 Vols. London 1747

Locke J. : <u>On Politics and Education</u> (Ed. Van Nostrand) New York 1947.

Machiavelli N. : <u>The Prince</u> Penguin Ed. (trans. G Bull) London 1961

Malebranche N. : <u>Treatise Concerning Search After Truth</u> (Eng ed.) 2 Vols. London 1694

Montaigne M. : <u>Les Essais</u> 2 Vols. (ed. P Coste) London 1724

Montaigne M. : <u>Oeuvres Complètes</u>, l'Integrale Editions du Seuil, Paris 1967

Montesquieu, Baron de : <u>Oeuvres Complètes</u> 8 Vols. Basle 1799 (C Louis de Secondat)

Nelson R. : <u>An Address to Persons of Quality and Estate</u> London 1828

Nicole P. : <u>Discourses</u> (trans. J Locke) (Ed. Hancock) London 1828

Pascal B. : <u>Pensees</u> (trans. A J Krailsheimer) Penguin ed. London 1966

Pemberton J. : <u>A View of Sir Isaac Newton's Philosophy</u> London 1728

Plato	:	*The Dialogues of Plato* O.U.P. (by B Jowett) 4 Vols. Oxford 1953
Pope A.	:	*Poetical Works* (Ed. H Davis) O.U.P. London 1966
Ray J.	:	*The Wisdom of God Manifested in the Works of Creation* Aberdeen 1777
Rousseau J J	:	*Emile or Education* (trans. de Monvel) Everyman Edition London 1963
Rousseau J J	:	*The Social Contract and Discourses* (trans. G D H Cole) Everyman Edition, London 1963
St Augustine	:	*City of God* (J W C Wand) O.U.P. London 1963
St John, H Viscount Bolingbroke	:	*A Collection of Political Tracts* London 1748
St John, H Viscount	:	*Letters on the Spirit of Patriotism: On the Idea of a Patriot King and on the State of Parties at the Accession of George I* London 1752
Saussure C. De	:	*Lettres et Voyages* 1725-29 Lausanne 1903
Shaftesbury, Lord (3rd Earl)	:	*A Letter Concerning Enthusiasm* London 1708
Shaftesbury, Lord (3rd Earl)	:	*Characteristics* etc., 3 Vols. London 1711
Skelton P	:	*Deism Revealed, or the Attack on Christianity Candidly Revealed* (2nd Ed.) London 1751
Smith A	:	*An Enquiry into the Nature and Causes of the Wealth of Nations* (4th Ed.) 3 Vols. London 1786
Smith A	:	*The Theory of Moral Sentiments* London 1759

Swift J : _Gulliver's Travels_ Everyman Ed. London 1940

Swift J : _Poetical Works_ (Ed. H Davis) O.U.P. London 1967

Swift J : _Satire and Personal Writings_ O.U.P. London 1967

Swift J : _The Tale of the Tub, the Battle of the Books and Other Satires_ Everyman Edition London 1970

Temple, Sir W : _An Essay Upon the Ancient and Modern Learning_ Oxford 1909

Temple, Sir W : _An Essay Upon the Origin and Nature of Government_ Ed. Works, London 1720

Temple, Sir W : _Observations Upon the United Provinces of the Netherlands_ 7th Ed. London 1705

The Craftsman: Saturday 29 January 1723, Vol IX London 1738

The Gentleman's Magazine or Monthly Intelligencer 1731 and 1732

The Spectator : 8th Ed. 8 Vols. London 1726 (by J Addison, R Steele etc)

The Tatler : The Lucubrations of Isaac Bickerstaff Esq., (Revised by the Author) 5 Vols London 1720 (by J Addison, R Steele etc)

Thompson J : _Poetical Works_ O.U.P. 1908

Thorold J : _A Short Examination of the Notions Advanced in a Date Book, entitled the Fable of the Bees or Private Vices, Public Benefits_ London 1726

Tindal M : _Christianity as Old as Creation_ London 1732

Voltaire F A de : _Candide or Optimism_ (trans. H Butt) Penguin Ed. 1947

Voltaire F A de : _Le Mondain_ Paris 1736

Voltaire F A de : Philosophical Dictionary (Ed. T Besterman)
London 1971

Ward E : The Character of a Covetous Citizen or a Ready Way to Get Riches   London 1702

Ward E : The History of the London Club, or the Citizens Pastime   London 1709

Ward E : The London Spy Compleat (in Eighteen Parts) 3rd Ed. London 1706

Wit J de : Fables, Moral and Political with Large Explications   London 1703

Wollaston W : The Religion of Nature Delineated   London 1722

Young E : Two Epistles to Mr Pope, Concerning the Ambitions of the Age   Dublin 1730

Young E : Love of Fame: The Universal Passion   2nd Ed. Dublin 1728

BIBLIOGRAPHY

PART III SOURCES 19th & 20th CENTURIES

Alexander Pope: Penguin Critical Anthology (Ed. F W Bateson & N A Joukovsky London 1971

Anderson P B : 'Bernard Mandeville on Gin', P.M.L.A. No. 54; 1939 pp. 775-784

Anderson P B : 'Splendour Out of Scandal, The Lucinda-Artesia Papers in the Female Tatler, Philosophical Quarterly pp. 286-300, 1936

Apters J P : 'Pope's To Bathurst and the Mandevillean State' Journal of English Literary History Vol. 25, 1958 pp. 23-42

Ashley M : England in the Seveneenth Century (1603-1714) Penguin London 1961

Bate W J : From Classic to Romantic: Premises of Taste in 18th Century England Harvard University Press Cambridge, Mass. 1946

Becker C : The Heavenly City of the Eighteenth Century Philosophers Yale University Press 1967

Bell J F : A History of Economic Thought New York 1953

E A Becker and M de P Lee : Selections from Bayle's Dictionary Princeton 1952

Blackstone W T: Francis Hutcheson and Contemporary Ethical Theory University of Georgia Monograph No.12 Athens USA 1965

Bonar J : Philosophy and Political Economy (3rd ed.) London 1922

Bredvold L I : The Intellectual Mileu of John Dryden University of Michigan Press, 1934

Bryson G : Man and Society: The Scottish Enquiry of the 18th Century   Princeton 1945

R E Butts and W F Davis : The Methodical Heritage of Newton Blackwell, Oxford 1970

Cambridge History of Literature   (Ed. Sir A Ward and A R Waller)
15 Vols. Cambridge 1949-63

Cannan E : Review of Economic Theory   London 1930

Cassirer E : The Philosophy of the Enlightment (trans. F Koellen and J Pettegrove) Princeton 1951

Catlin W B : Progress of Economics New York 1962

Chalk A F : 'Natural Law and the Rise of Economic Individualism' Journal of Political Economy Vol 59, 1951 pp 332-347

Chiasson E : 'Bernard Mandeville: A Reappraisal'   Philosophical Quarterly 1970 Vol. 49 pp. 489-519

Clifford J L (Ed.) : Man Versus Society in 18th Century Britain Cambridge University Press 1968

Courtines L P : Bayle's Relations with England and the English Columbia University Press New York 1938

Cohen I B : Franklin and Newton An Enquiry etc. Memoirs of the American Philosophical Society Vol. 43 Philadelphia 1956

Colman J : 'Bernard Mandeville and the Reality of Virtue', Philosophy 1972 Vol. XLVII, No. 180 pp. 125-139

Cook R I : Jonathan Swift as a Tory Pamphleteer   University of Washington Press 1967

Cragg C R   : Reason and Authority in the 18th Century
                    Cambridge 1964

Darwin C   : The Origin of the Species (6th Ed.) 2 Vols.
                    London 1890

D'Entreves A P   : Natural Law Hutchinson London 1967

Dewhurst K   : John Locke (1632-1704) Physician and Philosopher
                    A Medical Biography London 1963

Dixon P   : The World in the Early Eighteenth Century
                    1700-1740 Oxford 1959

Dobree B   : English Literature in the Early Eighteenth Century
                    1700-1740 Oxford 1959

Dobree B   : Variety of Ways: Discussions on Six Authors
                    Oxford 1932

Eddy, W A   : Introduction to Swift's Satires and Personal
                    Writings O.U.P. London 1932

Edwards T R   : Mandeville's Moral Prose, ELH XXXI 1964 pp. 195-
                    212

Encyclopedia Britannica   : Mandeville By BMM Vol. XVII 11 Ed.
                            Cambridge 1910

Encyclopedia of Philosophy : 'Bernard Mandeville' E Sprague;
                             Vol. 5 Free Press New York 1967

Encyclopedia of Philosophy : 'Egoism and Altruism' by A
                             MacIntyre, Vol. 2 Fress Press
                             New York 1967

Essays in Moral Philosphy : W K Frankenna 'Obligation and
                             Motivation in Recent Moral

Philosophy' (Ed. Medlin) Washington Press, Seattle 1958

Essays in Philosophical Psychology : (Ed. D F Gustafson) MacMillan, London 1970

Fichter J H : Roots of Economic Change London 1939

Foxon D : Libertine Literature in England 1660-1745 London 1964

Fussell P : The Rhetorical World of the Augustan Humanists Oxford 1965

Gauthier D P (Ed.) : Morality and Rational Self-Interest Prentice Hall, New Jersey 1970

George M D : London Life in the 18th Century Peregrine, London 1966

Gert B : 'Hobbes and Psychological Egoism': Journal of History of Ideas Vol. XXVIII, 1967 pp. 503-520

Gert B : Hobbes, Mechanism and Egoism, The Philosophical Quarterly Vol. 15 1065 pp. 341-349

C Gide & C Rist : A History of Economic Doctrines Harrap London 1948

Goldman L : The Philosophy of the Enlightenment, The Christian Burgers and the Enlightenment RKP London 1973

Goldsmith M M : Hobbes' Science of Politics Columbia University Press, New York 1966

Goldsmith M M : 'Introduction to' the Origin of Honour and the Usefulness f Christianity at War (2nd Ed.) Cass London 1971

Gough J : The Social Contract (2nd Ed.) Oxford 1957

Gray, Sir A : 'Adam Smith' <u>The Historical Association</u> London 1968

Gregiore F : '<u>Bernard de Mandeville et la Fable des Abeilles</u>' Nancy 1947

Halevy E : <u>The Growth of Philosophical Radicalism</u> (trans. M Morris) Faber, London 1952

Harth P : <u>Introduction to the Fable of the Bees</u> Penguin London 1970

Harth P : The Satirical Purpose of the Fable of the Bees, <u>Eighteenth Century Studies</u> II 1968/9 pp. 321-340

Hayek F A : 'Dr Bernard Mandeville' Lecture on a Master Mind, <u>Proceedings of the British Academy</u>. Volumme III, London 1966

Hayek F A : <u>Individualism and Economic Order</u>, R.K.P. London 1949

Hazard P : <u>The European Mind 1680-1715</u>, Pelican, London 1964

Hazard P : <u>European Thought in the Eighteenth Century</u>, Penguin, London 1965

Hearnshaw F J C : <u>The Social and Political Ideas of some Great French Thinkes of the Age of Reason</u>, Dawson, London 1967

Heckscher E F : <u>Mercantilism</u>, (trans, Shapiro) 2 Vols. London 1935

L Heilbroner & P Streeten : <u>The Great Economists</u>, Eyre and Spottiswood, London 1955

<u>Hobbes & Rousseau</u> : A Collection of Critical Essays (Ed. M Cranston & R S Peters) Anchor Doubleday, New York 1972

<u>Hobbes Studies</u> : (Ed. K Brown), Blackwell, Oxford 1965

Humphreys A R : The Augustan World, Methuen, London 1954

Humphreys A R : 'The Social Setting' and 'The Literary Scene' Penguin Guide to English Literature 4 from Dryden to Johnson London 1965

International Encyclopeadia of Social Sciences : 'Bernard Mandeville' by M M Goldsmith Vol. 9 Free Press, New York 1968

Jensen H : Motivation and Moral Sense in Francis Hutcheson's Ethical Theory (M Nijhoff) The Hague, 1971

Jack I : 'Samuel Butler and Hudibras' in Penguin Guide to English Literature 4 from Dryden to Johnson, London 1965

Jack J H : 'The Periodical Essayists' in Penguin Guide to English Literature 4 from Dryden to Johnson London 1965

Jefferson D W : An Approach to Swift in Penguin Guide to English Literature, 4, from Dryden to Johnson London 1965

Jonathan Swift : Penguin Critical Anthologies, (Ed. D Donoghue) London 1971

Johnson H : Predecessors of Adam Smith, New York 1937

Jones R F (et al) : The Background of the Battle of the Books, Stamford, California 1965

Kemp J : Ethical Naturalism MacMillan, London 1970

Keynes J M : The General Theory of Employment, Interest and Money MacMillan, London 1963

Kramnick I : Bolingbroke and His Circle, Oxford 1968

Lamprecht S P : Fable of the Bees, The Journal of Philosophy, Vol XXIII, 1926 pp. 561-579

Lecky W E H	:	History of European Morals from Augustus to Charlemagne, 2 Vols, 1869
Letwin W L	:	Origin of Scientific Economics, London 1963
Lovejoy A O	:	The Great Chain of Being. Study of the History of an Idea, Cambridge, Massachusetts 1936
Lovejoy A O	:	Reflections on Human Nature, The John Hopkins Press, Baltimore, 1968
McNeilly F S	:	The Anatomy of 'Leviathan' London 1968
McNeilly F S	:	'Egoism in Hobbes' The Philosophical Quarterly July 1966 Vol. 16 No. 64 pp. 193-206
MacPherson C B	:	The Political Theory of Possessive Individualism, Hobbes to Locke, Oxford 1970
Manuel F E	:	The Eighteenth Century Confronts the Gods, Harvard, 1959
Maxwell J C	:	'Ethics and Politics in Mandeville' Philosophy Vol. 26 1951, pp. 242-252
Mill J S	:	A System of Logic, Longmans, London 1967
Monro D H	:	A Guide to the British Moralists, Fontana, 1972
Morize A	:	Problems and Methods of Literary History, Boston 1922
Mossner E C	:	Bishop Butler and the Age of Reason, New York 1936
Mossner E C (ed)	:	'A Principle of Moral Estimation etc.' Journal of the History of Ideas, Vol. 21, 1960 pp. 222-232
Nagel T	:	The Possibility of Altruism, Oxford 1970

Nisbet R A : *Social Change and History*, O.U.P. New York 1970

Nishiyama C : *The Theory of Self-Love; An Essay in the Methodology of the Social Sciences, and especially Economics, with special reference to Bernard Mandeville*, Ph.D thesis, Chicago 1960

Novak M E : *Defoe and the Nature of Man* O.U.P. 1963

Novak M E : *Economics and the Fiction of Daniel Defoe*, University of California Press, Los Angeles 1962

Oakeshott M : 'The Moral Life in the Writings of Thomas Hobbes' in *Rationalism in Politics*, Methuen, London 1967

Orwell G : 'Politics V. Literature: An Examination of Gulliver's Travels' in *Inside the Whale and other essays*, Penguin, London 1957

Parsons C J : *Swift's Works 1710-1715 and Contemporary Ideas History and Histriography*, Ph.D. thesis, University of London 1968

Penguin Book of Eighteenth Century Verse: (Ed. D Dawson): Penguin, London 1973

Penguin Book of Satirical Verse (Ed. E Lucie-Smith) London 1967

Peters R S : *Hobbes*, Peregrine, London 1967

Peters R S : *The Concept of Motivation*. R.K.P. London 1969

Plumb J H : *England in the Eighteenth Century (1714-1815)* Penguin 1960, London

Plumb J H : *Growth of Political Stability in England 1675-1725*, Peregrine, London 1969

Pope and His Contemporaries Essasy Presented to G Sherburn : (Ed. J L Clifford and L A Landa) Oxford 1949

Popkin R H	:	'The High Road to Pyrrhonism' American Philosophical Quarterly, Vol. 2 1965 pp. 18-32
Popkin R H	:	The History of Scepticism from Erasmus to Descartes, Harper, New York 1964
Popkin R H	:	The Philosophy of the 16th and 17th Centuries The Free Press, New York, 1966
Popper C	:	The Open Society and its Enemies 2 Vols. Routledge, London 1966
Price M	:	To the Palace of Wisdom, Studies in Order and Energy from Dryden to Blake, New York 1964
Primer I	:	'Introduction to' the Fable of the Bees Capricorn, Ed. New York 1962
Realey C B	:	The London Journal and its Authors, 1720-1723 University of Kansas, 1935
Robertson J M	:	Essays Towards a Critical Method, London 1889
Robinson J	:	Economic Philosophy, New Thinkers' Library, London 1962
Rosenburg N	:	'Mandeville and Laissez-Faire' Journal of the History of Ideas, Vol. XXIV, No. 2 pp. 183-196
Rousseau G S	:	'Bernard Mandeville and the First Earl of Macclesfield Notes and Queries XVIII 1971 p. 335
Rex W	:	Essays on Pierre Bayle and Religious Controversy (Martinus Nijhoff) The Hague, 1965
Rude G	:	Paris and London in the 18th Century. Studies in Popular Protest, Fontana, London 1970
Russell B	:	History of Western Philosophy, Unwin, London 1961

Sampson R V : *Progress in the Age of Reason*, Heinemann, London 1956

Scheider L : 'Mandeville as a Forerunner of Modern Sociology' *Journal of the History of the Behavioural Sciences*, 1970, pp. 219-230

Schatz A : *L'Individualisme Economique et Social*, Paris 1907

Scott-Taggart M J : 'Mandeville: Cynic or Fool?' *The Philosophical Quarterly*, 1966 Vol. 116 No. 64 pp. 221-32

Shea J S : Introduction to Aesop Dress'd, Augustan Society Reprint No. 120 California, 1966

Atkin J S : *Readings in Early Anthropology*, Chicago 1965

Sociological Theory and Philosophical Analysis (Ed. D Emmet & A MacIntyre) MacMillan, London 1970

Spink J S : *French Free Thought from Gassendi to Voltaire* London 1960

Stark W : *The Ideal Foundations of Economic Thought*, London 1943

Stephen L : *English Thought in the 18th Century*, 2 Vols. Harbinger, 1962

Stephen L : *Essays on Free Thinking and Plainspeaking*, London 1873

Taylor O H : *A History of Economic Thought*, MacGraw Hill, New York 1960

Tuberville A D : *English Men and Manners in the 18th Century*, O.U.P.

Tucker G S : *Progress and Profits in British Economic Thoughts, 1650-1850*, Cambridge 1960

Vereker C : Eighteenth Century Optimism, Liverpool University Press, 1967

Vichert G S : A Critical Study of the English Works of Bernard Mandeville (1670-1753) Ph.D. thesis, University of London 1964

Vichert G S : Bernard Mandeville and a Dissertion Upon Drunkedness, Notes and Queries, Vol. 209, 1964 pp. 288-292

Viner J : The Long View and the Short, Free Press, Glencoe, Illinois, 1958 pp. 332-342

Von Leyden W : Seventeenth Century Metaphysics, Duckworth, London 1971

Warnock G J : Berkeley, Peregrine, London 1969

Watkins J W B : Hobbes's System of Ideas, Hutchinson, London 1965

Watt I : 'Defoe as Novelist' in Penguin Guide to English Literature 4, from Dryden to Johnson, Penguin, London 1965

Whitney L : Primitivism and the Idea of Progress, Baltimore 1934

White R J : The Anti-Philosophers, MacMillan, London 1970

Whitehead A N : Symbolism: Its Meaning and Effect, Cambridge 1958

Willey B : The Eighteenth Century Background, Peregrine, London 1964

Wilde N : 'Mandeville's Place in English Thought' Mind, Vol 7 1898

Winch P : The Idea of a Social Science, R.K.P., London 1967

Young J D : 'Mandeville: A Popularizer of Hobbes' Modern Language Notes LXXIV 1959 pp. 10-13.